T0193682

IT'S YOUR TIME, IT'S YOUR TURN

SONNY MARTELL

BALBOA.PRESS

A DIVISION OF HAY HOUSE

Balboa Press books may be ordered through booksellers or by contacting:

Balboa Press
A Division of Hay House
1663 Liberty Drive
Bloomington, IN 47403
www.balboapress.com
1 (877) 407-4847

Because of the dynamic nature of the Internet, any web addresses or links contained in this book may have changed since publication and may no longer be valid. The views expressed in this work are solely those of the author and do not necessarily reflect the views of the publisher, and the publisher hereby disclaims any responsibility for them.

The author of this book does not dispense medical advice or prescribe the use of any technique as a form of treatment for physical, emotional, or medical problems without the advice of a physician, either directly or indirectly. The intent of the author is only to offer information of a general nature to help you in your quest for emotional and spiritual well-being. In the event you use any of the information in this book for yourself, which is your constitutional right, the author and the publisher assume no responsibility for your actions.

Any people depicted in stock imagery provided by Getty Images are models, and such images are being used for illustrative purposes only. Certain stock imagery © Getty Images.

Print information available on the last page.

ISBN: 978-1-9822-4528-3 (sc)
ISBN: 978-1-9822-4530-6 (hc)
ISBN: 978-1-9822-4529-0 (e)

Library of Congress Control Number: 2020905310

Balboa Press rev. date: 06/08/2020

CONTENTS

INTRODUCTION

Imagine a life in which you do not worry about things in a way that causes you fear or uncertainty. A life where you know that everything is going to be alright no matter what the circumstance is. Imagine that all you have to do is think of something and it will happen for you as if it was magic. And what if your relationships and family life were truly happy and fulfilled? Then most importantly, imagine a life in which you are truly happy with yourself and with who you are and who you are. This book is going to give you the tools and the knowledge to all of this and more. The only unknown for you after you read this book is whether you are going to take the time to practice the techniques you are going to learn, and if you believe you are worthy of all that is available to you in the world. You have taken the first step by opening the book and begin reading it. The only thing that can stop you now is you.

I was fortunate to learn this at a very young age. I did not have a father growing up, my mother was poor, we did not have any luxuries, and I did not come from an abnormally positive household. It does not matter what your childhood was like. What your background is. What your ethnicity is. Where you live or grew up. It does not matter what you have done or what has happened to you in your life up until now. Tomorrow is a new day and you can make tomorrow any way you wish. You can change your life immediately. The knowledge, secrets and techniques are all in this book. This book is now in your hands. Therefore, the knowledge is now yours. You can do whatever you choose with it. Just know that it does not matter who you are, there are no reasons that everything that is described in this book can happen for you. There are no exceptions to this rule. Anyone can do it if they believe they can and do what it takes to achieve it.

What is even more exciting is that it's easy and fun to practice what it takes and the results you will achieve will be immediate.

Once you realize that there are no boundaries to your life and happiness, and that you have all of the secrets to everything you have ever wanted right inside of you, you will never be the same. So often we look at the world around us as our guide and how we measure ourselves. Rarely do we take the time to look inside ourselves. And very rarely do we look deep inside ourselves. Many people are afraid of what they see when they look inside so they stop doing it. But the feeling when you do not like yourself never really goes away, no matter how much you try to ignore it. The same is true if you have the feeling that you are not good enough or that you do not deserve or have what it takes to have what you want the most in life. People become afraid to want things and take risks because they are afraid of failure. Sometimes they stop dreaming altogether. Imagine a life in which the word failure does not mean that you have not achieved something, but instead it means that have tried something and are that much closer to what you want. Imagine a life in which failure is a positive word. You can imagine that now because that is exactly what failure will become to you. You will no longer be afraid of failure.

As you read this book take the time to look around you and notice just how fascinating the world is. So many things were invented and imagined by humans. We have so much and so many conveniences and things around us at all times. Humans lived in caves not too long ago. Now we have vehicles that can go to space carrying humans which can live in them for months and longer at a time. We have vehicles that are traveling through space looking at other planets and for existence of life beyond our galaxy. I can go on and on talking about the things that are available to us today that humans invented. The point is that all of these ideas were imagined and dreamed of, then invented. Inventions are just one example of how humans dream and change the world we live in as well their own world every day.

You will realize as you progress through your own journey in life that people that seem to have it all in life are not just lucky. Once you understand that there are certain specific things everyone can learn and practice to shape their reality and their life in any way they wish, your life will change forever. A switch will go off inside and you will understand something that is inside of everyone. Some people spend their time beating themselves up and tearing themselves down while some people lift themselves up. Then there are those that just float through life and seem to be flat and have no sense of direction. The beautiful thing about life and being a human is that we get to decide how we want to live our life. We are our own best friend or our own worst enemy. The key to life is to make sure you are your own best friend. And to achieve a positive attitude.

The main focus of It's Your Time, It's Your Turn is achieving a positive mental attitude. Think of this as the basis for all good in everyone's life at all times. The word, "Positive" is going to be written often and in every chapter. Positive is only a word until you understand what it really means. This book explains what having a positive attitude really means. It explains exactly how to achieve a positive attitude and explains all that happens to someone's life once they achieve a positive attitude. The main goal you should have while reading this book and practicing the techniques in it is to practice all of the things together and achieve a complete and balanced positive attitude as well as a complete and balanced life. You are about to learn all of the tools you need to succeed. But with any tools you have to use them to build the life you wish to have. It's Your It's Your Turn was written for you to become the person you have always wanted to become. To have the things you want in life. And to achieve the life you have always dreamed of. This book makes it fun and easy to understand and practice. It is a guide for every aspect of your life. For every aspect of each day from the time you wake up until the time you go to sleep every night. This book was writing for you to do whatever you want with. While you read the book do not feel pressure or a sense of failure if you are not doing the things in the book or if you have not understood the things in this book.

With most things in life, you will realize that the difference between success and failure is a very thin line and most people quit right before they succeed. Therefore, they don't realize how easy it really is to succeed and not fail when they try something. Once you learn how to stick with an idea or situation that you choose to partake in long enough to achieve it or see it through your mind body and soul will become in tune with all of your thoughts and goals. You will become a true being of happiness and achievement. So many other things will also open up for you in your life. Just the sense of happiness and wellbeing you are going to achieve is priceless, but you are going receive so much more if you practice all of the techniques in this book.

The greatest part of all this is that once you learn how to put all the techniques of achieving a positive attitude together you then get to use them in any way you wish. There is no right or wrong so don't overthink the chapters or yourself while you are reading. Just read and understand and practice. Feel the transformation and enjoy it. Know that the transformation is only what you choose it to be. You are in control of every part of your life. Trust in your faith as well and know that you are not alone in your journey. You will learn how to tap into the energy around you at all times. The energy from others and the energy from the universe, but only if you choose to open up to it. It is completely your choice and decision to make.

It's Your Time, It's Your Turn was purposely written to be understood simply and easily. I have made the techniques simple to understand and easy and fun to practice by. What you will realize after reading the entire book and practicing all of the techniques together is that the big picture of what will happen inside you will be nothing short of extraordinary. With that being said, expect extraordinary things during and after reading this book. You are extraordinary and need to expect nothing short of living and extraordinary life, no matter what that means to you. You will see immediate results as you read each chapter and practice the techniques. This book was written so you can open your eyes for the first time and see what is really happening around you every day as you go through life. You will see things and feel things that you never have. You will feel different, better, happier and more confident then you every have after you start practicing the techniques, all while staying true to your values. That is what this book was written for.

While you are reading this book, give yourself much credit and be proud of yourself that you have chosen to do something to better your life, as well as to better the lives of those around you. Every secret to having it all is at your fingertips in this book. The secret to how your body mind and soul function together to become in tune and you can harness the positive energy inside of you will be yours to use in any way you chose now.

As you read this book make it your main goal to achieve a positive attitude at all times in your life. Simplify what you want to get out of this book to just that. Then once you understand what it takes to achieve this goal, pick the most important techniques that apply to your life and your goals in life and focus on them to understand them completely and focus on mastering them. Once you start practicing the techniques and taking time for yourself you will never feel the same again. You will have a sense of wellbeing and happiness that you have never felt before. Your confidence will rise and everything about your sense of wellbeing is going to become more defined and pronounced. Let this positive energy happen inside of you while you are reading and practicing the techniques in this book. Welcome the positive energy and positive changes that are going to happen for you. Tell yourself that you deserve to be happy and positive. Tell yourself that you are worthy of having whatever you desire. And tell yourself that it's your time and it's your turn to enjoy and live your life to the fullest.

The main thing to remember while reading this book is that you are going to start to feel different physically and mentally in a positive way. You will start to feel the change immediately as you read each chapter and practice what you learn in each chapter. Embrace this feeling and don't fight it. Remember that you are reading this book to get all you can out of it. People around you may notice a change in you. Your attitude, the way you talk, your body language. Don't be embarrassed of this become self-conscious, especially if the people that notice ask you what you have been doing differently or why you are acting differently than you normally do. This is perfectly normal and will pass quickly. Feel free and happy to tell them that you are practicing being more positive and are practicing having a positive attitude. You will see that everyone you know wishes they were more positive and wants to know the secrets you are going to learn in this book. Once you start practicing what you learn in this book and others will be drawn to you and you will notice the difference immediately. Embrace this feeling and don't fight it. Enjoy it and seek more by learning more and practicing more. And most importantly, be very proud of yourself for taking the time to better yourself and take some time for yourself. The time you take to learn and practice the techniques in this book are going to affect the people around you, your loved ones and your family in a positive way. You are going to better their lives as well so be proud and excited about the decision you have made to read this book. Now get started, embrace your knowledge and never look back!

Chapter 1

Time to Change Your Thoughts

It's Your Time, It's Your Turn was written in hopes that it would inspire and help people to live their lives to the fullest. The world can be a negative place, and people can have a hard time dealing with the negativity that surrounds them. Achieving a positive attitude is not taught in schools, in colleges, or anywhere else. Instead, we are taught how to deal with society in other ways, but we are left by ourselves when it comes to dealing with positivity and negativity. Positive thoughts are the catalyst for true happiness, health, success, good relationships, dealing with society, as well as everything else that affects our lives. A positive attitude is what helps us cope with all that life throws at us daily, weekly, monthly, and yearly. It will be explained exactly why this is as you read each chapter.

The more you learn how to deal with positive and negative thoughts and actions in your life, the easier life can become to understand. Things can begin to become clear as to what path is the right path. Choices will become clearer as well, and you will know that you are always making the correct decisions as you become a positive thinker. Realize from this day forward that the journey to achieving a positive attitude is one like no other. This journey will involve you feeling things that you have never felt before. The things you will learn and practice in this book are going to light fires inside of you that you did not know existed. You are going to feel things you have never felt before. These feelings are going to give you a sense of joy and happiness, but the key to it all is that you are going to learn how to have these feelings and emotions at all times, twenty-four hours a day. Your waking hours will be better. Your sleep will improve. Your dreams will improve. Every aspect of your life is going to be affected in a positive way after you learn and start practicing the techniques in this book.

There is a lot of positive-thinking and self-help material in the world, but it is up to everyone to seek it out and learn about it. It is up to you to decide that you are going to take the time to learn about a positive attitude and self-help techniques. No one will force you to do this in your lifetime. Each day we are forced to learn new tasks at our jobs, about life, and many other things. We are constantly taking the time to learn about life. Now it is time for people to learn about the key that will unlock the doors for them. This is the key that many people do know about but do not take the time to share because either they are too busy leading their own lives or they do not think of taking the time to share their secret. It is the key to overcoming fears, doubts, and anxiety. It is the key to happier relationships, friendships, better health and having all the things you want in life.

I am happy that you are about to take the time to learn about these techniques and that you are either beginning your journey to a better life or enhancing the journey you have already begun by reading this book. I have spent a lifetime learning about people and positive thinking. I have taken the time to study my own emotions and how others react to positive and negative thoughts. I understand how a positive attitude can influence everyone around us. Positive thinking is the key to a happy life. There are other factors that must be dealt with in order to lead a full and happy life, but if you are positive most of the time, you will have the roots and the catalyst for everything else you want out of life. A positive attitude will help you feel better mentally, physically, and emotionally. A positive attitude will help you to achieve your goals and your dreams.

We all want more out of life; some people just do not know how to get it. A lot of people wonder why there are people that achieve all their goals and are happy most of the time. They cannot seem to get their life together and fall short when they attempt to do things. This is because they have trained themselves to be this way. The good news is that we can all train ourselves to be any way we want to quick and easily. It takes discipline and effort, but it is absolutely attainable. We can train ourselves to push through negative thoughts that have stopped us from achieving things that we have wanted to achieve in the past. All we have to do is take the time to learn how and then practice it. Once we learn these techniques, we can then practice them more and become better at them. As we practice these techniques more throughout our lives, we can then learn how to become the person we truly desire to be. We can then learn how to have the things in life we desire. It all starts with a positive attitude and a positive lifestyle.

We must also learn how to deal with all the negativity that surrounds us at all times. And we must learn how to deal with our own negativity. There are always going to be negative people and negative situations that we will encounter daily. It is how we choose to deal with these encounters that separates the positive person from the negative person. This is how it works. This is how simple it really is. It is such a simple concept, but the way this is achieved is a complex thing, and it is something that must be practiced repeatedly. We cannot simply wake up one day and undo what we have learned in a lifetime. The exciting news though is that we can do whatever we want in life because it is our life to live. We can choose to become whoever we want to be, and we can choose to have whatever we want. All we have to do is learn how to get it. This is a fun and easy process.

If you take the time to notice the people around you that have the things in life that you would like to have, you will realize that they are of all ages, nationalities, and races. You will realize that they are women and men and they are from all walks of life. What is the common thread in these people? If you take the time to analyze them and get to know them, you will see that the common thread is how they think. It is how they view their world and how they view others. These are the common threads. Yes, there are other factors that will come into play, but for the most part, how people think is the difference between people. For some people, they were programmed to be positive from their parents when they were children. For others, there have been events in their lives that have forced them to realize this secret to being positive. And for others, they have just taken the time to learn and change their thinking. The exciting news is that you too can do this anytime you choose to. It does not matter what your past was like, how you were raised by your parents, or how you have spent your life until this point. All that matters is what you are going to do today that will affect your tomorrow. Yesterday has already passed, and today is here. Tomorrow is your unknown. You can make tomorrow whatever you want. You can make tomorrow anything you want. It is your tomorrow; all you have to do is decide what it is going to be like, and it will be that way.

Before you proceed reading this book, have paper and a pen by you. Also, make sure you have a marker to mark interesting sentences and chapters in this book so you can go back later and review things you find interesting. Make this book like a workbook for you to look at later. Hopefully this book will inspire you to learn more about positive thinking. My journey began many years ago, and your journey may be beginning today. Remember as you are reading this book that this is all real. Think of the things you are going to read about in this book as a behind-the-scenes look at a life many people only dream of. It is like being at a magic show and being behind the curtain, knowing what is happening with each illusion and each trick. The only difference is that this is real life and there are no tricks about what you will read in this book and the magic show is in your head. It is real, and it is happening around you every day. You probably know people that are practicing all the techniques that are in this book and more.

As you move through the chapters in this book, do not become overwhelmed with all the things you are going to read about and learn. Go at your own pace and take your time. If you need to read a chapter more than one time and practice what is in the chapter for a while before you decide to read the next chapter, that is perfectly all right. Go back and reread the previous chapter before going to the next chapter if you take a while to move from chapter to chapter. You will see that each chapter leads to the next with more knowledge and more techniques. There is no right or wrong pace to read this book.

As you are reading this book, buy another book about positive thinking so you are armed and ready to read about more ideas and more techniques immediately after finishing this book and practicing all the techniques you will learn. This will reinforce the techniques and ideas that you learn in this book as well as teach you others to begin practicing. You will notice that you develop a craving for more positive material and more positivity in your life. It will become infectious, and you will begin to feel good in a way you may have never felt in your life. Or you may have felt this way before, only to have it slip out of your hands and make you wonder why you cannot feel this way all the time. You will begin to realize that you can feel this way all the time. If you begin to feel overwhelmed as you are reading this book, it is perfectly normal. You cannot change overnight what took you a lifetime to become. If you begin to feel overwhelmed, all you have to do is understand that this is your subconscious telling you that you are thinking and acting differently than you always have. It is trying to warn you to take notice of your actions because they are not how you normally act. This is perfectly normal, and as you decide to make a change in your life more and more, you will feel less resistance from within yourself.

Once I began thinking about writing this book, it was obvious to me that I needed to do it. I often thought about how many lives I could affect by sharing the things I have learned about positive thinking and achieving a positive attitude. As you are reading this book, keep in mind that I have learned most of these things by practicing them for myself. I studied people and authors and positive speakers, but without choosing to practice these techniques and learn how they would affect my life, there would have been no changes made in my own life. I have also discovered and practiced my own techniques to achieve a positive attitude. These techniques and ideas will also be shared with you. There are so many things that will stem and branch from exploring and practicing and achieving a positive attitude for yourself. It must become a lifelong commitment. I had to take the time to see how being positive through all my ventures in life as well as certain negative things that have happened throughout my life led me on paths that took me to great places. I began to learn that trusting in these thoughts and paths would result in my life becoming fulfilled beyond my wildest dreams. I also learned the most important side effect to achieving a positive attitude, inner peace. You will have to take the time to practice these techniques and others you will learn repeatedly until you realize what paths they are going to lead you on.

As you read this book, just know that "life is going to get in the way." This is also perfectly normal. If you remember to stay as consistent as possible in thinking positively and practicing positive-thinking techniques, you will win the race. There have been times in my life that I have fallen and had to get back up. I have slipped into thinking negative thoughts, and I have let my fears get the best of me. It happens to everyone. You will begin to realize as you learn more about having a positive attitude that most successful, happy people have become this way because they have fallen and gotten back up more than most people. They have not let themselves become afraid of failure and falling down. It is time for you too to move past fears and failures and learn that these things are part of leading a normal life. Falling and getting back up is a positive experience, not a negative one. Life does get in the way sometimes because we all have lives, and our lives are constantly changing. We are always growing and changing as we move throughout life's journey. This book will help you to realize that your journey through life is just that, a journey.

Now it is time for you to buckle up and go on a wild ride into your thoughts and into your dreams. I hope that you enjoy this ride as you read this book because "it's your time, it's your turn." Remember this as you read this book. Make this time your time to become the person you want to and to have all that you want in life! It is important that you write down all your thoughts that will be presented to you in this book throughout each chapter. You will be asked to write down certain sentences and sayings in each chapter. Do not take these for granted. Once you are finished with this book you will have compiled a list of positive thoughts and sayings that will be like no other. Once all of the positive saying and thoughts are combined into one list and you practice your list you will become unstoppable and you will achieve a sense of self- fulfillment and happiness that you have never felt before. It is important that you look at these thoughts every day and that you believe that they are going to happen for you. Writing your thoughts and goals down on paper and looking at them every day is the key to your success. Remember this as you read this book. Do not feel embarrassed about your thoughts and dreams. Be proud to share them with anyone you choose to. Be proud of yourself and know that you are doing the right thing.

How exciting it is for you that you are going to take the first step or take another step closer to a truly fulfilled life. I hope that this book brings you much happiness and helps you to achieve all your goals in life. I can only hope that this book will teach you many things or at least one thing or one idea that will serve as a catalyst for you to achieve all that you desire in your life, both spiritually and monetarily.

We all have a destiny and a purpose. I have been destined to write this book my entire life. When I was in high school, I realized that I was happier than most of the other kids. The other kids would often tell me, "You are so happy all the time, don't you get down sometimes?" I never did get down and noticed that the other kids did quite often. I did not think much about it at the time, and when I met kids that were not happy all the time, I would just make them feel better. This has lasted my entire life. My positivity is what was contagious. It was my smile, because I always had one on my face.

It was my body language, my attitude, but it all came from having a positive attitude. I always thought positive thoughts.

What was it that made me be happy all the time? Was I born with it? Are we born with it? Did I develop it? Do we develop it? I was not raised to have a positive attitude, came from a poor household, had only a mother, no father and did not have much growing up. The one major thing I did every day, and still do today every day is make a conscious decision to have a positive attitude, which programs my subconscious to make that happen. It is really that simple. But the process in which this happens and what will transpire in your life as it happens and after it happens is nothing short of amazing. One thing that I do know for certain though is that everyone wants to be happy all the time. I know that we absolutely can be happy all the time if we choose to be. And I also know that there are too many people in the world that are not happy all the time. There are also those that are unhappy most of the time and do not know why. There are those people that do not get what they want, yet they want so much. There are people that say they are always unlucky. It is like a disease in our society. We all know it; we all see it. It is the sea of negativity. Am I describing you? Am I describing people you know?

What I want you to do right now is put down the book and just take a minute of silence and close your eyes. Think about this moment, and tell yourself, "Today is the day I start making a change." Don't be hard on yourself, and don't think about much. Just tell yourself that today is the day. Go ahead, do it.

What is the secret? Is there a secret to happiness, money, love, finding God, health, and more? Yes, there is a secret to all these things. But it is not what you think. It is not some complicated formula or some mysterious thing. It is as easy as understanding who we are and who you are. You must want to make this change, or it will not happen. That is another secret. When you put the book down and told yourself that you were going to start making a change today, did you mean it? Did you really mean it, or did you say to yourself something like "I don't know if I can do this" or "I don't know if this is going to work"? If you did not believe it completely and feel it in your gut, then try again. Put the book back down and do it again. If you are not convinced that today is the day that you are going to change your life, then don't be hard on yourself. Let it go. What I want you to do is start reading this book every time by closing your eyes and telling yourself that today is the day you begin changing your life until you know without a shadow of a doubt that you mean it. It's that simple. It's step one of all of it. This will do two things. It will truly be the beginning of your new life, and it will teach you the basis of everything you will need to know to achieve what you want in life. You must be true to yourself. Say this out loud, "I have to be true to myself." To achieve what you will learn in this book, you must learn to believe that you can achieve it, and you must truly want to achieve it. An alcoholic or drug attic cannot turn their life around until they truly decide it is time to do so. The negative thinker cannot develop a positive attitude and become a positive thinker until they decide they are going to achieve it. It is that serious.

In this book you will say things out loud, you will write things down, and you will even scream things. You need to learn how to write things down sometimes. There is a certain part of your brain that remembers things and reacts in a "now action" state. Take a thought and pick up a pen and write it down on a piece of paper. It makes what you are trying to accomplish much more powerful. Do not underestimate the power of writing things down. Have you ever noticed that successful people are always writing things down? If you have not, take notice and you will see.

There is one very important thing among all the things you will read in this book that you are going to have to remember. Maybe you should write this down. Firstly, don't be afraid to write in this book. It is your book. Tell yourself that you are going to read it again someday, and write in it. Underline things in it. So, what are you going to have to remember? You need to remember that changing your life does not happen with reading one book. No matter how good I write this book and no matter how much you know it is true and how much you get out of it, you are going to have to read other books. You are going to have to change many things that you are probably doing in order to become a more positive, happier person.

People do not like change but look at these changes as something you are going to have fun doing. You are going to have to learn how to do these things, and guess what? You are going to have to continue to learn for the rest of your life. It is ongoing, not just a one-book seminar. The first big mistake people make is to read a book, go to a seminar, or try to get more positive and then tell themselves that they cannot do it because it doesn't work for them. You know those people that are happy all the time, are successful, and have the nice things in life? Those that have the things you want, no matter what it is? They practice at it every day. Now put this book down again, and put a big fat smile on your face. Be very happy with yourself. Feel good about yourself, and give yourself a mental pat on the back. Why, because today is the day you are going to *start* making that fun and exciting change. You know it may not happen overnight, but now you know that it starts here. Smile big, and smile at yourself. Now do it. Put the book down!

Did that feel good? It felt great, didn't it? Now you must figure out how to have that feeling all the time, every day, all day. What you must realize is that life can try to get you down. There are so many things that can happen every day that can get us down. Life brings challenges, doesn't it? Again, there is another trick to dealing with these challenges. It is how we look at them. Yes, it's that simple. What will not be that simple for you is to do it consistently and to believe what I am saying. Until you do the things you will learn in this book enough times to believe that they work because you see it happen for yourself, you may not believe that they do work. I understand that. I was the same way as you are. We are all the same. Practice will make perfect in this case. Tell yourself right now that you are going to do these things until you see them work for yourself. Go ahead. Write it down, and then put the book down for a minute and tell yourself that you are going to do that. I also want you to observe others that are successful, however you see success, and are happy all the time. You notice that I said, "However you see success and happiness"? This is your life and your world to live in however you choose. Do not be fooled by TV, commercials, the internet, news, and movies. Do not be fooled by society. Live your life how you want to live it. Observe people that always get what they want. You will see a lot of similarities between them and the things that I describe in this book. That will speed up the process in you believing that you can do it too. If I can write about it and you read it and you can practice it and you can observe others doing it, then it can happen for you too, can't it? You must tell yourself, "If others can do it, I can too." You also must tell yourself, "I deserve it." You do deserve it.

Reading is just one of the ways that you will need to practice in your new life and the new you. Reading is among the most important though. Reading sinks into our subconscious, which we will learn about later. Reading makes magic happen in our brain. Beware of what you read. What you put into your brain will be remembered. Reading is a great way to speed up the process of being more positive. Always be reading a positive-energy or self-help book. You will get to the point where you know and practice most of the techniques in the book, but there will always be something in each book you read that will make you say, "Hmmm, I never thought of that." You will probably learn many things from each book, but if you only get one thing out of it, it will be worth the read. I always get at least one thing out of a self-help book that I read that makes me a better person. That is all I am looking for. Don't expect miracles. Just keep reading them. You will see what I am talking about. When I say keep reading them, I don't mean for the next couple of months or a year. I mean for the rest of your life. Save your books, and read them over again as time goes by. You see things in them that you did not see the first time. I guarantee it. Reading positive material will be one of the most important changes for you to make. Read positive articles if you like the newspaper. *Do not read negative articles.* If you like magazines, read positive stories in them. *Do not read negative stories.* If you like reading on the Internet, read positive material. Watch positive shows on TV and positive movies.

Start being aware of yourself after today. Start observing yourself. Start doing some soul-searching. You are going to have to decide who you are, who you want to be, and who is inside your body. Maybe you are happy with yourself, but you want to be more positive. Maybe you like your life, but there are changes in certain areas that you would like to make better. The beauty of becoming a better you is that you get to do it in any way you choose. Give yourself a break. You are not that bad. You are amazing. Do some soul-searching and start discovering who you are. Take some time for yourself. It is important. You are going to begin your journey today to liking who you are. This is very important, and you need to remember it. Write it down. You cannot make others happy until you make yourself happy. You cannot be happy around others until you are happy around yourself. Such simple sayings, but so powerful. You need to learn to be happy with you. It is the essential beginning of being a positive person and getting what you want in life. Think about it. If you are not happy with yourself, how can you be happy at all, and how can you get what you want? When you are unhappy with yourself, you most likely make people around you unhappy too. Look at people that are always happy. When they are around others, they become happy as well. It is like a positive virus. Too bad there is no such thing as a positive virus. Think of your new life as a positive virus. First you are going to get infected with it, then you are going to infect others with it. That is right—someday you will become the teacher and help others be better.

Think of yourself as a person that is now on a fun and exciting journey to complete happiness. You are going to have to practice at it, but just know that it's fun and easy to do once you learn how. Why are we so fascinated with movie stars, professional athletes, singers? They strive for perfection. Some are naturals, and some just practice, practice, practice. Either way though, what do they have in common? They strive to be the best, and they are always practicing. Most athletes, movie stars, and singers have been doing it since they were little children. Their parents supported them from a young age. They get better and better and never stop practicing, do they? They become so good that they get to call themselves professional. You must become a professional positive thinker. It doesn't matter if you are born with it or if you must practice, practice, practice. You just must decide that you are going to do it. Think about this for a minute. It doesn't cost money to become happier and change your life. You don't need a degree for it. Yet it is one of the hardest things we must do in our lives.

Time to let you in on another secret. It is so hard to be happy and positive all the time because society is negative by nature. Take a look around you. Commercials on TV are negative, the news is negative, the internet is negative, people talk about negative things, and much more. We are constantly bombarded with negativity. And what I am about to tell you is frightening. This happens from the moment we are born. There is a word that babies learn from day one, "no." The word "no" becomes a negative force in our life from the day we are born. I am not saying that we cannot say "no" to our children or to others as adults, but I am trying to make you think outside the box. "No" is a negative word. What about when people tell us we cannot do things? What about when we see beautiful people on the cover of magazines? What about when we watch TV shows and commercials and people have things that we want in those commercials, but we tell ourselves that we will never have them? There is so much negativity around us since the day we are born. So here is my point. If it took a lifetime to get where you are now, then how long do you think is it going to take you to think positively all the time and be happy all the time? Let me tell you. It is going to take some time and practice to change a lifetime of programming and negativity. That is right—I said programming. You are going to have to reprogram yourself. It sounds technical and complex, but it is simple. This programming begins the second you decide to have a positive attitude and have all that comes with it.

Here is something to remember. Grab your pen and paper. "What you believe, you will achieve." It is really that simple. Your brain remembers what you put in it. You will learn more about this in later chapters and how to master the techniques that will help you change your programming. Another thing that you will learn is that you have the power to change whatever you want in your life. Yes, it is true. But you must start by believing it. Put the book down again. Take a minute and tell yourself, "I can change whatever I want to." This exercise is the same as the others. It will not work until you believe what you are saying to yourself. If you put the book down and said it to yourself, "Yeh right, sure, that will work," then guess what? It won't work. Put the book down again, and now really believe it. If you still don't, do not beat yourself up over it. Just keep saying it to yourself until you believe it. I bet if you keep saying it to yourself, you will start believing it! I will explain why in later chapters.

Now that you have begun your journey, it is time to start feeling good about yourself. You need to be proud that you have chosen to read a book like this. That you have taken the time to do something for yourself. When you begin harnessing the power within you, it will become addictive, and you will crave more. Make sure that you satisfy that craving. Always be feeding it. Take time to think about positivity in everything that you do all day and night long. It may not work at first all the time. How could it? You are learning how to do something that you are not accustomed to doing all the time. And now that you know it will not happen overnight, it is something that you are going to work at for a lifetime. You don't have to be hard on yourself. But you do have to try to be consistent. Consistency is the key here now. Believe me when I tell you. I have been working on being a positive person my entire life, and I have only begun to kick it into high gear. At age forty-four I feel like it is only the beginning. It does not matter if you are young or old; it only matters that you start now.

There will be times when you are challenged, and there will be times when you fall back down from being positive. Why do you think everyone makes such a big deal out of good and evil? The hero and the villain? People make movies about it, the newspaper writes about it, the news reports it. There is something inside of all of us that always gives us the choice to speak, think, and act on good things or bad things. Have you ever noticed that? For some reason, society is infatuated with negative things. There are movie stars that have wonderful lives, everything people want, but people love to hear about the bad things that happen to them. The news reports on catastrophes, shootings, robberies, killings, and all kinds of bad things that happen to people. Why is that? I will tell you why. It is a deep, dark hole that people can fall into. It also makes people feel better to talk about others and to see bad things happen to others, so they think. They think it does not make their lives look so bad. Think of it like a drug addict or alcoholic that must do drugs or drink every day to feel better. That is kind of what it is like. I will explain why in later chapters. Now think about what it would be like to always talk good about others, not worry about catastrophes and shootings and the bad things that happen to others. What would it be like to live in a world that was free of all that? It would be different, wouldn't it? That can be your new world. And with it will come opportunities, achievements, and happiness that you have only dreamed of.

We all know that there is no such thing as a perfect world and that negativity is part of life. We also know that imperfection is everywhere. You are going to have to learn to embrace imperfection. Imperfection is what makes life so interesting. Embracing imperfection is a positive action. Just think about how boring the world would be if there was no imperfection. Nothing would go wrong. There would be no challenges. Everything as we know it would be completely different. Imperfection is what makes humans. It is very important that you start realizing this right now. No one is perfect. And you are not either, so while you are learning how not to be so hard on people, don't be so hard on yourself. Only be hard on yourself when you are not being positive. Being negative from this point forward is a no-no. You must hold yourself accountable, but now you are going to learn how to be confident and calm, knowing that you are headed in the right direction. You are going to have that something everyone is searching for and everyone wants. And you are going to use it for good things.

This book is going to talk about every aspect of your life. It is going to be packed with techniques to help you be who you want to be and have the things you want in life. If you have read other self-help books and been to seminars, then get ready because this book will talk about some things that they have not. If this is your first book ever on self-help and you have never been to a seminar or listened to a CD, then get ready because you are about to go on a wild ride. It's time you learn how to get in touch with your soul, mind, and gut and get them in sync. So, let's get started right now!

CHAPTER 2

How Our Brains Work

Have you ever wondered how a computer is made to function? You put an enormous amount of information in it, and it stores it. Then you put more and more in it. Some people put many different types of information in their computers, don't they? But most people put the same type of information in their computers? Companies take information that is pertinent to their company and put all their data into their computers as the years go by. Then when they work on their computers, that information is used in various ways for the company and its employees to accomplish what they want to, right? Your brain is like that. What a revelation. The computer was invented by a human. The computer is like a brain. Here is the thing. A computer cannot come close to doing things that your brain can.

From the day we are born, we put information into our brains and become the person we are today, don't we? It is very important for you to understand what I am about to tell you. Your brain is like a computer, but it has something a computer does not. Your brain is always being programmed. It gets programmed through your subconscious and your conscious minds. The quicker you understand and embrace this, the quicker you will realize that you can become and have anything you want in life. What you put into your brain every day is what is going to stay in there. Things go into your subconscious mind, and guess what your subconscious mind does? It goes to work to accomplish what is in there. It never stops. It never sleeps. The great news about this is that you have programmed your brain up until this point, haven't you? So that means you can now reprogram your mind if you want to. Maybe you do not want to reprogram you mind. Maybe you like yourself just the way you are. Good for you. If I was with you right now, I would say to you, "Congratulations, liking yourself the way you are is the number one goal in life." But if you would like to make some serious changes about yourself or your life—be a better person, have more, do more, be more positive, be happier, and help others—you may have to start by reprogramming your mind.

So how do we reprogram our minds? First and foremost, we watch what we put into it. And we must remember that programming our minds is something that we do consciously, which will work through our subconscious. Cool, right? It is a trick that once you learn, it's yours forever. Programming your mind is the same thing as telling yourself that you are going to be positive all the time or telling yourself that you are going to change your life. If you do not believe it, it will not happen. Everything you learn in this book will not work if you do not believe it will. That is step one. Once you see one thing happen to you that is talked about, you will then believe that it all works. Start by doing this though. Until it happens to you, look at someone that is how you want to be. Observe them for a while. Just take a look at how they talk. Look at their face, their eyes, their body language. Observe them. Listen to what they talk about. Listen to the tone in their voice. They practice being who they are. You will see it. You practice being who you are too. Now you are going to have to practice differently if you are not getting the results you want. You may have to reprogram your brain. This does not mean that you are going to be someone that you are not. You should always keep your values and your beliefs. Don't change who you are. Just reprogram yourself to positive mental attitude and to be happy all the time, and everything else will fall into place. It really is that simple.

How do you get started reprogramming your mind? You get started right now. It is time to put the book back down. Get a piece of paper and your pen. Not the piece of paper you have been taking notes on, but a blank piece of paper. Write on the paper that you are going to change your life today. Today is the day that you change your life. Write down that you are going to think positively and that you are going to reprogram your mind to have the things you want and to become the person you want to be. Write down that you are a good person and that you are ready to make a change. Write that you deserve to have the things that you want in life. Write down that your relationships with your family and with people you know are going to become better. Now write down some things that you would like to reprogram about yourself. Then put the date on it. Put the book down and think about it for a little while. Write it down. Think about it tomorrow and the next day and the next weeks and months to come. Add to the list, and redo the list as it becomes more defined.

Now you have a working list that will start defining what you want from life and how you are going to get it. When you think of something and then write it down, it goes from your conscious to your subconscious. Get it? You want to learn how to get thoughts that you want into your subconscious. Your subconscious is like an ant that has been buried under a pile of sand. It digs and digs to get out of the sand until it does. It does not stop until it gets what it wants. Now that you know this, it is time to start putting the list you made into your subconscious. You already started doing that by writing it down, but now you must look at that list every morning when you wake up and every night before you go to bed. If you work in an office, make a copy of the list and look at it throughout the day. If you don't work at a desk, put it in your purse or your wallet and look at it when you go to lunch. But the most important time that you need to look at the list is before bed. When you look at your list before bed, it will get to your subconscious while you sleep. Then when you wake up and look at it again, you will assure your subconscious that it is the right way to start your day and that you are headed in the right direction while programming yourself.

So how does the subconscious work besides like an ant trying to get out of a pile of sand? Have you ever felt something was not right, but you could not figure it out? Did you feel it in your gut? Your subconscious did that to you. Your subconscious is part of your inner spirit. It is that thing in the background running all the time that you cannot put your finger on but know is there. Your subconscious is not your spirit; your spirit is everywhere in your body, and its many functions are all connected. If you are not in touch with them, then you are going to have to learn how to become in touch with them. The first step though is to reprogram your subconscious. It will start the ball rolling and be the catalyst for everything. When you begin seeing results from understanding how to program your mind through your subconscious, you will understand how your entire body works. Your brain is called the brain for a reason, is it not? The definition of a brain is "the part of the nervous system in vertebrates that is enclosed within the skull, is connected with the spinal cord, and is composed of gray matter and white matter. It is the control center of the central nervous system, receiving sensory impulses from the rest of the body, and transmitting motor impulses for the regulation of voluntary movement. The brain also contains the centers of consciousness, thought, language, and emotion."

When you think about something repeatedly, it usually happens, doesn't it? What you must learn is that you must practice thinking about what you want repeatedly. This is how much you are going to have to think about it. You are going to have to think about these things seven days a week, all your waking hours if it something that is very important for you to become or to have. That is what "over and over" means. Once you write what you want down on a piece of paper and then look at it first thing in the morning, throughout the day, and before you go to bed, you will then see that you start thinking about your list all the time. As time goes by and you master this technique, you will learn how to do this without reviewing a list throughout the day and before you go to bed and the first thing when you wake up. Think about how long a doctor must go to school for. They must complete four years of undergraduate to get that degree, then complete four more years of medical school, and then complete three to seven years of residency training. Why so much schooling? And until they complete that schooling they cannot be on their own. Can you imagine how much programming a doctor has had to know everything about the human body and how it functions in all those years of studying? How many years do we have to go to school before we are considered an adult and become part of society that can function on our own without the supervision of an adult? These rules and laws are put in place because all this schooling is programming people's conscious minds and subconscious minds to be part of society or to become a doctor and be able to practice what they learned. I make a list of what I want, who I want to be, and how I want my relationships to go every December, before New Year's Eve, and hang the list on my bathroom mirror. The list has a six- and twelve-month plan on it. Then I look at the list day and night and analyze where I am at and how I am going to achieve the list. When I make a list every year, I believe that I am going to get what is on that list, and I have been doing this for twenty-five years. I have programmed myself to believe and achieve my lists. If I fall short of some of the things on my list, I just add them to the next year's list. You may be at the beginning of your journey. How exciting it is for you that you are learning this secret. You should have a huge smile on your face right now. You should have an excited feeling in your stomach that you have figured out a simple thing that not many people know about, which will change your life forever if practiced. Just this one bit of knowledge, if practiced and mastered can have an immediate positive impact on your life.

Professional athletes know this, actors and actresses know this, famous singers know this, and successful entrepreneurs know this. People in happy, loving relationships know this. They all have this in common. Believe me when I tell you. They all have thought about what they wanted for many years, if not their entire lives, and most were probably taught to write it down and review it. What have professional athletes been doing since they were children? They practice their sport, and they also practice something else. They have a playbook or a game plan that they are constantly practicing repeatedly every day as a team. The greatest athletes go home after practice and dream about being a pro athlete as they have been doing since they were children. They vision themselves winning the big game, making the crucial turnover, doing something that makes their team win it all. An actor goes to classes and learns how to act, but the great ones go home every day and aspire to be the best actor of all. They look in the mirror constantly and act. They practice lines and pay special attention to their faces, their body language, the tone of their voice, and many other things. This is also what successful businesspeople do. They go home after their day is done and think of ways to improve their businesses, and they set goals for their businesses so they will achieve what they want. They lie awake at night thinking of how they can make their business better and how they can make themselves better. They think about how they can improve their work environment get more production out of their employees to achieve their common goals. People that have successful relationships and families think of their family's night and day and program themselves to be a good partner and parent. People that have jobs are constantly programming themselves how to master their careers and be a better employee to achieve their goals within their corporations.

What if you do not aspire to be an actor or an entrepreneur? No problem. Those are just examples of successful careers and lives that many people would like to have. What if you aspire to try not to work very much and have more free time? What if you aspire to donate all your time to a charity and you do not care about money, fame, or success? Maybe that is success to you. Maybe your idea of success is staying home and raising children. Your subconscious will help you achieve whatever you want—whatever you want out of life. The only thing the subconscious mind gives is what you want. Understand this. Your subconscious mind does not care how you program it. It does not work better if you want to be a movie star or professional athlete. It is your brain, and you get to program it however you wish. The only thing you may have not known is that you are constantly programming your mind. And you have been programming your mind from the day you were born.

Now that you know this, it is time to start reprogramming. You have learned how to define what you want and how to put it into your subconscious. Now you know that you can program your mind to have whatever you want and that it is a fast and easy process. Now it is time to understand something very important that you need to know. This process happens in different time frames for everyone. Everyone is different. But it is achievable for every human being on earth. Believing this will happen and can happen is the key, but knowing that mastering this technique may take time is the secret to its success. It took me years to truly master this technique. And I am still, twenty-five years later, working on it. Also, life will throw curveballs at you. Things will happen that will sidetrack you. We do not live in a perfect world, remember? Things happen that we do not anticipate and cannot control, don't they? You will have times when you do not work on programming your mind. You may forget for a while to do this. You may have a year that something happens in your life that is so serious that you forget to program every day. Do not beat yourself up over this. We are human. Just know that when you stop programming your brain how you want, you take a small step backward. It is like good and evil. That is why there is good and evil in the world. You must remember that everything around you constantly are kind of negative. There is a lot of positive in the world, but you must seek it out, see it and become it. You know the saying "You are only as good as the company you keep"? How about "You are what you eat"? Well, what about "You are what you put into your brain"? People really don't like to talk like that, but that is what these saying are for—for what you are putting into your body and your brain.

Part of reprogramming yourself is going to have to incorporate not only what you do privately and by yourself but how you change the world you live in. Look at the people you would like to emulate, the same people you looked at, and observe how they talk, walk, act, look. Observe the world they create. What do they do while working at the office? What are their habits? What do they do after work?

Where do they go? Who do they hang around with? I bet you will find out they hang around other people that are like them. I bet they go places and do things that they consider to be good for their lives. Are you doing that? Have you really thought about this? Everything you do during your waking hours and when you sleep is programming your brain. This sounds a little over the top, doesn't it? Well, it is over the top. It's how you get to the top. It's what the most successful people in our society have learned. Does this mean you have to go out tomorrow and get rid of your friends and stop doing the things that you do and going to the places you go? No, it does not, but you are going to need to analyze these things in the next months and years. If you truly want to make a change in reprogramming your subconscious mind, you are going to have to probably change your surroundings as well. Someday you will be the person that others observe and try to figure out what is special about. Maybe you then will share the techniques you have taught yourself with others.

Do you have friends that talk about other people all the time in a negative manner? Do you watch the news when you get home from work? Do you talk negatively about your job and the people you work with to your spouse or mate? Do you watch reality shows and wish your life was like the people on TV? When you are at work, do you talk badly about your company or your supervisors with other people? When you get home, do you think about your day and say to yourself, "I had a terrible day today. It was rough, and I am tired and don't like my job and the people I work with"? What do you do after work? Do you eat food that is bad for you and then sit and watch TV shows that are bad for you? Do you spend your time off from work doing things that you know you should not be doing? Think about it. All these things start adding up. Do you wake up and say to yourself, "I really don't want to go to work today," then turn on the news, get in the shower, and say to yourself, "I wish I could stay in bed this morning, and I didn't have to get ready for work?" Then get in the car and start your drive that you do every day on the way to work, saying, "I hate traffic" and "This drive is so boring," then pull in at your job and park, saying to yourself, "I wish I didn't have to go in here today" or "I hate my job." You may think about the people that you do not like or your boss or that you do not have a sense of pride in your job. Then you go into work and start your day. Most people sit at their desk saying to themselves, "I want more from life," "I wish I could do something else," and things like that. Then when you go on break, you go with someone else and talk about negative things the entire time. Do you talk about your boss, the job, your life? You do the same thing at lunchtime. Then when it is time to go home, you walk out of the door of your job and say, "I will see you tomorrow." Then you get in the car, tell yourself how you hate the traffic on the way home or how boring it is to go on the same drive every day, and drive home. Before bed, do you think about going to work the next day and how you wish you did not have to? On your days off from work, do you do anything fun for yourself? Do you hang around positive people or negative people? Do you do positive things or negative things on your day off? Do you spend your day cleaning your house and wishing you were doing something else?

Now the picture should be becoming clear in your mind. That is how your brain gets programmed, first and foremost by how you think and what you think about, but it is also by how you act and who and where you hang around every day. It is a combination of everything you do every day. It is also a part of what you do when you sleep. Are you sleeping comfortably? Is your room ideal for you to sleep how you would like to? Now you are probably seeing the whole picture. You must really change your life and reprogram your brain by being positive and doing the things you consider are good for you all the time. This can seem overwhelming right now, but once you do this and see the results, you will say to yourself, "Why haven't I been doing this my entire life?" Once you see how it works firsthand, you will experience something that you only dreamed of. Your life can become like a dream. You may have to pinch yourself. Again, everyone achieves this at their own pace, so do not expect this to happen overnight, but do expect it to happen because it will, and most importantly, do not be hard on yourself. Be proud of yourself for doing something. And life has its ups and downs, so always remember that setbacks are part of the process. It is not that you will have setbacks; it is how you will handle them when they come.

As you begin reprogramming your mind, you will need to learn how to think positive thoughts, even in negative situations. This is one of the most challenging parts of reprogramming your mind. When something bad happens to you or when there is a situation to have a negative thought, which will be often, you have to take that negative thought that you are used to thinking or saying and make it a positive thought. Always tell yourself that it is going to be all right. Say it often. "It is going to be all right. Everything is going to be all right." Say it and believe it when you have trying times, and everything will be all right. If you think about it, when you have had hard times in your life, they had always been handled one way or another, and you always got through them. Why not be positive while going through hard times? Once you do this, you will understand the power of being positive. Once you program your mind to be positive, negative things that happen to you will not seem so bad anymore. Why, because your subconscious mind will be busy trying to find all the positive things going on and coming out of the negative situation. Powerful stuff, right? That is what successful people know that you may not. Have you ever known someone that went through something bad and handled it well? Have you ever seen people that have things happen to them that you would think are bad and they do not make a big deal out of it? That is because they are always telling themselves it is going to be all right. This is the same as all the other techniques I have described so far though. It only works if you really believe it. You must believe that it will be all right. The trick is just to keep telling yourself that it will be all right repeatedly. This sounds so simple, but doing it and believing it are not as easy as it sounds, right? Try it. When you are going through something bad, just keep telling yourself that it will be all right. Your subconscious will start believing it, and you will start believing it. You will then begin seeing the positive points of a bad situation and the scale will begin tipping in your mind to see more positive things happening instead of only the negative.

There is another way to believe everything will be all right. You need to find an inner place in your body, mind, and soul—a peaceful place where you feel calm, relaxed, and assured that everything will be all right. Learn how to find that place in your body. It is like meditating, but you do not have to sit with your legs crossed and your thumb and pinkie finger touching each other. It is something that you can do when you are alone. You just must start learning how to find and develop that place. It is not a place that I can pinpoint for you because you must find it yourself. You will know when you find it. You start by taking a moment when you are alone and in a quiet place. Clear your mind. Maybe you should close your eyes, but you do not have to. Concentrate on clearing your mind. Try to feel a sense of well-being come over you. Then tell yourself that everything will be all right. Tell yourself that your world is good and that you are happy and that good things happen to you. Then do something that a lot of people forget to do but successful and happy people are good at doing. Do nothing and relax. Just relax, and soak in the positive thoughts you whispered to yourself. It is a great way to program your mind to relax and to be positive at the same time. Do this often and get good at it and find your happy place. That is why people fool around and say, "I am going into my happy place." We really do have one. It is vital to find and master that happy place. That happy place will help program your subconscious to make your world a happy world.

When you start learning how to reprogram your mind, you will have to start using a different vocabulary also. As you reprogram your mind longer, you will find yourself using these words more, but at first you will have to force yourself to use them. Some of these words are "amazing," "terrific," "outstanding," "awesome," "great," "perfect," "fantastic," "excellent," "good." When someone asks you how you are doing, answer them, "Terrific" or "Outstanding" or "Fantastic." You will start believing it, and it will help reprogram your subconscious. When you describe others, use the words "awesome or "wonderful." It sounds so corny at first, but you will get used to it. When you use these words to describe things and people, pay close attention after you say them at how you feel and how the person you say them to reacts. Watch their eyes. They will light up when they hear these words. You will feel better when you use these words. Start thinking of other words that you would like to say that are awesome and positive. Listen to other people when they talk, and when they say a word or use a phrase that makes you feel good, remember it and start using that word or phrase when you have the chance.

Now I know the picture is crystal clear to you as to how this whole reprogramming thing works. I know I have talked a lot about reprogramming. It almost sounds like you are about to become a completely different person. Well, you are about to become a different person. You will keep your morals and the basic foundation of who you are. That will not change, unless you want it to. But reprogramming your mind for happiness and success is not as dramatic as it sounds, is it? It is not such a big deal. It is a well-kept secret that happy, wealthy, successful, healthy people know about. The most important thing for you to remember is that everyone does this at their own pace. And you are going to have to practice at it all the time. And you are going to have to get good at it. And you are going to have some setbacks. Learn to deal with them, and do not be hard on yourself. Just keep at it, and get better at it.

Another thing that you are going to have to learn is that everything happens for a reason. You must program your subconscious to believe this. It will give you an inner sense of calmness and well-being that you have never felt before. When bad things happen to you and you tell yourself that everything happens for a reason or, better yet, when you get to the point that you do not have to tell yourself because your subconscious mind is programmed, you will see solutions to problems much faster and clearer. God has a plan for all of us. By knowing this, it will make all your decisions the right decisions, even if they do not turn out well. There is always a reason for things you do. You may not know why yet, but you always find out later, don't you? How many times have you thought you have made a bad decision only to find out that good came of it? What if you went into all your decisions knowing that something good will come out of them no matter how they turn out? When bad things happen to us, we become stronger, better, wiser, and that much closer to success. Write this down. Sink it into your subconscious. Write down that everything happens for a reason. Sink this into your subconscious. Your subconscious loves to learn things like this.

OK, so let's tie all this subconscious stuff together. There is an end result to reprogramming your subconscious besides just being happy all the time. When you have positive energy running through your brain and your body all the time, something magical happens. Do you know that you are made up of mostly water and protein? We all know that we are full of organs that function together. And we all know that we are full of hormones. If you do not know this, it is all right. Our bodies are making chemical reactions constantly. According to scientists, approximately 37 billion chemical reactions happen in our bodies per second. That is how we do everything that we do all day, even how we sleep. It is how we breathe, see, smell, touch, move, and feel things. If you think negatively and are unhappy all the time, it affects all of you. All your senses. Your hormones. Everything. That is what you become. The same goes if you think positively and are happy all the time. When you stress out, feel fear, worry, feel incompetent, ugly, overweight, sad, and all those emotions, it comes from your subconscious. You have programmed yourself to be that. Yes, some people legitimately have chemical imbalances in their brains that make it impossible to just reprogram themselves, but most people just need to adjust their thinking. Your brain has convinced you of who you are. Now it is time to feel how wonderful and amazing and terrific and awesome and incredible it can feel to have positive energy running through you and releasing hormones that will make you feel fantastic all the time! You can feel happy, confident, relaxed, good-looking, and all those great things that you want to feel. When your subconscious is unleashed to be positive all the time, it will open doors for you and make you feel amazing. It will tell your conscious mind and your body to act and to start achieving the things you want out of life. You will be compelled to start doing more and living a better life.

CHAPTER 3

The Power Of A Positive Attitude

By now you are fully aware that this book is about achieving a positive attitude. But there is so much more to it than that. It starts with positive thinking, and then it branches off into many other positive aspects of your life. Positive thinking is just a term. What happens inside of you and outside of you when you exercise this term is the real thing you are after. Do not let people fool you into thinking that a positive attitude is not the way to live your life. And do not let people tell you that positive thinking is corny or weird. That is their insecurities and their negativity talking. Your friends and family will notice a change in you as you start practicing the techniques in the chapters and start looking and talking more positive. What you will be so excited about, though, is what is going on internally and externally in your body due to the positive thinking. Unless someone experiences it for themselves, it is hard to imagine what it will do to them. Think about feeling good all the time. Think about smiling all the time. When you do have a pain, you do not really worry about it because you tell yourself that you are strong, and then it goes away. When something bad happens to you, you do not sit around and dwell on it until it makes you feel sick in your stomach, and you can't breathe correctly, and you lose sleep over it. You know that it is going to be all right. And then it really is all right. That is what people are not going to know about you becoming a positive person. Remember this. You will see that I am right about what your friends and family notice about you as time goes by. But when they realize this is the new you someday, they will become like a moth drawn to a bright, hot light. This may be as you are reading or immediately after you read this book, or it may be a little time after you read the book. Everyone is different. Do not be hard on yourself. Just be consistent and know that it is going to happen for you because it will.

A positive attitude will lead to many other great things for you. When you are positive, your boss will be more likely to give you a raise. You will be more likely to get a promotion. You will be more likely to get picked for a position within your company over others. Positiveness will lead to you getting jobs that you apply for over others. You be happier at work then you have ever been. A positive attitude will let you make decisions to start your own business rather than talk yourself out of it. When you are positive, you will feel better physically. You will have more energy. You will feel less stressed when you are positive. You will want to do things that you like more. Your relationships with your friends and family will be dramatically better when you are positive. Your relationship with your children will be better. Your relationship with God will be better when you are positive. All your decisions will be the right decision, even if they seem like the wrong decision, when you are positive. We use the term "positive thinking," but it really means much more than that, doesn't it? Think of your new life as a new lifestyle. It is going to become a way of life. It is going to be the new you. Positivity will change every aspect of your life. And it will change other people's lives as you teach them what you have learned.

What is the power of positivity? When you reprogram your subconscious to be positive and you are consciously always being positive, strange and wonderful things will happen. The way you view life now will become different. The way you view people and the world will become different. What this does is open opportunities for you. That is how those annoyingly happy people get what they want all the time. You will have many chances each day to be negative. Just wait until tomorrow and see if I am wrong. It is what you do each time you can be negative that will start to count. When you get in a situation where you can be negative, you must consciously be positive at first. You must get to the point that you always remember to turn negative talk and situations into positive ones. Even if you start being negative and then realize it and then be positive, then end the situation on a positive note, you have done it! You were positive. Practice this all day and night, every day and every night. Someday it will become a subconscious function, and you will no longer have to remember how to do it.

Some other way being positive all the time will affect your life is that you become a much happier person. You may say, "I am already a happy person." What if you were a happier person? You probably have never felt what it feels like to become a truly positive person. When you do not engage in negative thoughts, talk, and actions, you will find yourself smiling a lot more. You will find yourself laughing a lot more. When you smile, it releases endorphins immediately in your body. Endorphins are chemicals in your brain that are released that cause you to feel happy, reduce stress, and boost your immune system, among other good things. Just a smile can do all that. Imagine if you smile all the time. Everything about being positive and happy is good. You must understand this. There is nothing that is negative about being positive and happy. It is all good for you. Some studies have shown that laughing also releases endorphins and has the same effect as smiling, but even better. Learn to laugh often.

When you think positively, it makes you happy and makes you smile and makes you laugh often. When you laugh often, it makes you happy and makes you be positive and makes you smile. When you smile, it makes you think positive and laugh and be happy often. Do you get it? It is all intertwined. It all goes together. Then when you do all these things all the time, your mental health gets better, and your physical health gets better also. It just happens. You are going to have to feel it for yourself, but the proof is in the pudding.

Remember those people you started observing? I bet they do not call in work often. I bet if you observe them outside work, they are active and do things they like to do often. I bet that they are healthy too. I am not saying that you will never get the flu or a cold again, but I am saying that you will feel better, much better. This is the beauty of positive thinking.

Now you know why I write the word "positive" so much. It is not a weird word. It is not a crazy word. It is not a silly word for weird people to talk about. It is a fantastic word! One you need to get into your vocabulary. Say it out loud, "Positive." Say it right now, "I am going to be a positive person." The reason I keep using the word "positive" over and over is because I want to keep it simple. The journey you face to become positive all the time will be simple too if you take the time to practice, and the prize you seek is simple as well. It is one word, "positive." Everything else will fall into place once you achieve the goal. That is how it works. It just works that way. It is a part of the human body that is a well-kept secret. As a matter of fact, the world usually tends to go the other way— "negative." That is why it is so hard to be positive all the time. Do you think that if since you were born everything around you was positive, everyone said positive things, no one talked negatively about one another, the news only reported positive events, commercials on TV told you that you were a great person, TV shows and movies did not have anything negative in them, and your work environment was a completely positive place, you would have to practice being positive? Of course not. You would be practicing it every day, right?

Now that you know the secret to being positive all the time, it is time to start practicing it and using it. It's time for you to make your world a positive world, no matter what is happening around you. First though, you are going to have to convince yourself that it will work. Talk to other positive people about this. If you drink a lot of alcohol and go to bars, you tend to meet and hang out with people that drink all the time. If you go to the gym all the time, you will meet people that work out like you do. You will probably hang around other people that work out. If you have a hobby flying model planes, you will most likely end up hanging out with other people that do the same thing. If you love watching sports, then you will hang out with people that like sports. If your children are your life, you end up hanging around people that have children. Start trying to hang around people that are positive and happy all the time. That is right. I said it. You may even have to make new friends. Do not stop being friends with the friends you have now. But if your friends are not positive and happy all the time, seek new friends that you can start interacting with. You will see in them all the traits I have described and more. You will see where you are headed. It will be strange at first. You won't know what to say in conversations that are positive and then lead to other positive topics. It will seem weird at first, but you will get the hang of it after a while. You will see how much they smile and laugh. Their smiles will be pure and honest and warm, and their laughter will be real, not fake. Listen for the difference. Pay attention to it. Watch how much different it is to be around positive people. Look into their eyes. See how bright and shiny their eyes are. Watch how they look at other people. Look the energy they exude as they talk with others.

When you think positive all the time, you will begin to get a sense of confidence that you have never felt before. It will always be in you. It will be like having a shield around you. You will feel stronger, both physically and mentally. Of course, it is no mystery why. I explained it. Your body will be releasing chemicals and hormones that make this happen. That is what our bodies do. That is the anatomy of a human being. Now that you know this, you get to make the choice as to how you want to use your mind and body.

I have talked to people that told me that they enjoy being negative. I know that they would much rather be positive, and they know that they would much rather be positive, but they choose to be negative, and they speak it out loud. They program themselves to be negative and even tell themselves they enjoy it. They choose to use their body and mind in a negative manner. We all know people like this. When you are around people like this, try to be positive after they speak their negative thoughts. Watch what will happen to them. They will notice what you are doing. They will like it. They will respond to it. It can become fun to watch someone try to have a negative conversation with someone that will not engage in it.

I will sometimes be with people that are having a negative conversation. They may be talking about other people or how bad life in general is. You know how conversations like that go. When it is my turn to talk, I will often talk about a certain good quality in the person or the people we are talking about. Or I will bring up a positive thing that we are talking about. It is a subtle move that I make, but I will not engage in the negativity. Most of the time, after it is my turn to talk two or three times, I can get the group to start talking about positive things. They will still throw in some negative chatter, but when I will not engage in it, there is always someone else in the group that would much rather be having a positive conversation and will join in, which will sway the group more. This technique is not easy to do. You must be strong, and you must be consistent and quick on your feet. But here is what will happen eventually to you. While people in a group are having a negative conversation, you will not really be listening to the negative talk when you have reprogrammed your mind and have become a positive person. Your subconscious will tune it out. After all, you have taught your subconscious to be a positive mind. That is also why it is so hard to be positive when you have taught yourself to be negative your whole life. While people are talking negatively about other people and the world, my mind is busy thinking about good things. When I respond in a conversation, I naturally will respond in a positive manner. It is just who I am.

Do not think for one minute that I am Mr. Perfect. I am not. I have negative thoughts and even will speak negatively. I am not perfect. If I were, I would be the richest man in the world. Everyone would want to study me and be like me. The only thing that I do differently is make a conscious effort to be a better me with positive energy and positive thinking constantly. I am aware and understand the benefits of having a positive attitude because I practice it every day and speak with others about it often. I have felt what positive thinking will do for me. I have lived all these things I have described so far. I have also lived and experienced all the things I will describe in later chapters. Everything came to me through positive thinking. It is the power of positivity.

When I was a teenager, I did not understand that I was a positive person, but I programmed my mind at a young age to be positive without knowing it. Then something incredible happened to me. In my early twenties, I began reading positive-thinking and self-help books. I read sales books, which are self-help books also. I went to seminars on how to be a better person. I hung around positive people that were ahead of me and knew these secrets of positivity. I was a positive person already, but when I began studying it and learning how to master reprogramming my mind and practicing these techniques, it went to an entirely different level. That is the level I want you to achieve. Once you experience the true power of positivity, you will know it.

Yes, I still have negative thoughts. I have fears. I have doubts. I talk negatively sometimes. But I make sure to limit it, and I never engage in these emotions for very long. I had doubts about writing this book. What do we naturally say to ourselves? "If I write this book, people may not like it." "If I write this book, I may be wasting my time." "I do not want to waste my precious time on writing a book that people will not like." But I wrote it, didn't I? I could have easily let those thoughts stop me. So easily, but I did not. I moved past them. We will talk about how to move past doubts and fears in later chapters, but for now, just know that I did exactly that. I moved past the negative thoughts. And once I moved past them, I never looked back. That is the pure power of having a positive attitude. Firstly, positive thinking will let you dream up good things to do for your life. Secondly, positive thinking will allow you to achieve those dreams because you will not allow yourself to become overwhelmed with negative thoughts. It will allow you to figure out what you need to do to get what you want. It will help you overcome the obstacles. This is what successful people know that you do not. It sounds simple when I describe it, doesn't it? You just think positively, and all your fears go away, and you achieve what you want in life. Well, it really is that simple. All that you have to do is get your brain to the state that this happens automatically. It will be programmed for happiness and success. It can and will happen for you.

I once joined tae kwon do for about a year and a half. I became a green belt and was on my way to a brown belt, which is before a black belt. My teacher was a chief master, but I did not know it. He was a man that had done pretty much nothing but tae kwon do his entire life. He was in his fifties, about five feet eight inches tall, in great shape, quiet, respectful, and not someone you would want to make upset. After about a year and a half of studying tae kwon do under this man, he finally talked me into going to a competition. I would always find a way not to go to the competitions because I did not join tae kwon do to compete in competitions. I wanted to get some exercise and learn self-defense at the same time. It just sounded fun, and I went and joined up one day because it was close to my house. Then one day I was out of excuses. I knew that I had to go to the next competition. My teacher was very patient with me for a year and a half, but he gave that look that someone like him gives one of his students when he does not have an option to not do what he wants. I knew my number was up. So, I told him that I would go the competition.

When I arrived at the competition, it was exactly like I thought it would be. There was a sea of small children and teenagers in white tae kwon do outfits. I was one of the few adults that were there to compete and not watch my child compete. Then the opening ceremony began. Yes, there is an opening ceremony to a tae kwon do event.

Some of the men and women that were also dressed in their tae kwon do attire walked up to the front of the event where they had a very long row of tables set up with white tablecloths on them. In the middle of the table was a podium with a microphone. It turned out that these adults at the table were the other instructors of tae kwon do schools in my city. One man walked up to the podium and announced, "We are going to begin the ceremony." Immediately, all the people in the room, including the parents, stood to attention and turned toward the tables at the front of the event center, and the competitors, including me, lined up in rows across the event center. This was a huge place with hundreds of people in it. The entire center came to a dead quiet. You could have heard a pin drop in the place. Then the man at the podium said, "Please be seated." Everyone in the room sat down on the floor with their legs crossed. The ceremony started, and as a ceremony before a tae kwon do event should go, there was cool Asian music and recognition of things and instructions and then introductions. One by one different people at the table took turns going to the podium and moved through certain aspects of the opening ceremony. They were taking turns on talking by rank. As they introduced themselves, I realized that their rankings as instructors and black belts were going higher and higher.

Then one man walked up to the podium and announced with authority, "And now, it is my great honor to introduce eight-time black belt Chief Master Yoon and Mrs. Yoon." Suddenly this very diplomatic, cool music started playing, the kind with the trumpets. Then out of nowhere, from the side of the building, my teacher came out. Everyone else in the building knew where to look, but I did not. He was dressed in a tuxedo, and his wife, who sat at the little desk every night at practice, Mrs. Yoon, was dressed in a black evening gown like she was going to a wedding. She had her hair done, her nails done, and makeup on. These people were in white tae kwon do outfits every night I saw them. And they did not have shoes on. When they started walking out, everyone stood and then bowed. Everyone in the room. I was shocked. "This was my teacher for a year and a half," I said to myself. I could not believe my eyes. Then they both walked to the podium, and again the man introduced Chief Master Yoon and went through his list of credentials. He went on and on telling everyone things I did not know about the man I spent an hour with twice a week for a year and a half, and he ended by saying, "And Chief Master Yoon will be at the table at the side of the room after the competition for autographs." My teacher was the head of the entire city. He was the highest-ranking chief masters in the American Tae Kwon Do Association. This was my teacher and his wife. Then Mr. Yoon stepped to the podium and sternly said a couple of words—a couple of chants that everyone else knew but I did not—and said, "Let the competition begin." Wow, what a sight that was. I will never forget it. And I did get his autograph on a T-shirt I brought.

When I went to tae kwon do to practice every night with my eight-time-black-belt chief master teacher, we learned the art of tae kwon do. Chief Master Yoon never told me who he was. He never had to give me his credentials. Every night when practice started, we always did the same thing. We stretched saying the same things, we warmed up saying the same thing, and we began practice doing the same thing. We began practice by doing the same moves and kicks repeatedly every night. There would be times when we would mix it up a little, but for the most part, the practice sessions went the same. Mr. Yoon would spend time teaching us the philosophy of tae kwon do, but for the most part, it was the same kicks and techniques repeatedly. Those techniques would become more advanced and longer as we moved up from one belt to another. It could take four or five or even six months to achieve the next belt.

Mr. Yoon would add moves to the techniques, and as we began moving to the higher belts, we began learning more self-defense and more sparring techniques. We began sparring more. Once the sparring began, Mr. Yoon would explain to us that we were being prepared to learn the art of self-defense. He explained that the early belts were there to teach the basis of the moves and techniques of tae kwon do. He explained that we did the same thing over and over all the time because we were making the reactions in our bodies with defense moves, kicks, and strikes automatic if we ever were to be in a situation that we had to use them. He explained to us that tae kwon do is the art of self-defense, but it is achieved by not having to think in the event of a fight. The mind and body should automatically be prepared to strike and defend from strikes while immobilizing our opponent and simultaneously using the techniques learned in each situation that may arise. There were many throws, kicks, grabs, and strikes that we learned and many ways to defend ourselves if someone tried to grab us or hit us. We could instantly defend ourselves and either grab them to submit them or kick them or strike them. We worked on these moves repeatedly. Someone would come at us and try to attack us, and we would defend. But it all started in the earlier practices with basic kicks and strikes being done repeatedly. We still practiced those moves over and over but also began using those moves to spar.

One of the main ways you would move to a higher belt in tae kwon do was demonstrating that you could automatically, without thinking, defend against an attack and then throw the strikes, kicks, grabs, and throws learned for that belt. If you could not automatically do these things, you did not pass to the next belt. So, what was happening in tae kwon do every night? We were programming our minds to learn self-defense. We were programming our minds to learn the tae kwon do art of self-defense. There are many martial art disciplines. The tae kwon do office just happened to be close to my house at the time. I could have been involved in karate, mixed martial arts, kickboxing, judo, etc. It would have been the same thing every day, just different techniques and moves and philosophies. We were being programmed for the event that someone would attack us. No matter which way they came after us, even if they had a weapon, Mr. Yoon was programming our minds to think and defend ourselves with our bodies, no matter what circumstance we found ourselves in. Yes, we were being programmed. That is what martial art is. It is programming your mind in a certain discipline to defend yourself in the techniques that the discipline teaches. You achieve this by doing the same moves over and repeatedly. Mr. Yoon would tell us that was the goal we were trying to achieve. Reacting without thinking was what every practice session was getting us closer to.

This is very interesting, is it not? The oldest culture on earth has been practicing this since the beginning. Also, while we were learning all this self-defense, Mr. Yoon was also teaching us how not to get involved in a fight. He always taught the little children in the class that using the techniques was a last resort and that the reason we learn tae kwon do was to give us confidence, so we did not have to use it. Mr. Yoon would spend a lot of time teaching the young children why they should not fight and why they should respect other people and their parents. I understood what was going on, but I was always fascinated to hear him teach and to watch the beauty of Mr. Yoon programming the minds of young children to become better people and more respectful and confident. The little kids even had a chant that they had to do before every practice would start and at every belt ceremony. They had to stand up and face the parents each time, and the chant stated that they would be respectful toward others and that they would listen to their parents. The parents knew what was happening, and now that you know the power of programming your mind, you can only imagine how that affected the children over time.

Now let's talk about something that is fascinating. I enrolled in tae kwon do about nine years prior to writing this book. I was pretty good at it too. But now, nine years later, if my life depended on it, I could not remember any of the techniques I learned. They have all left my brain. If someone were to attack me, I would not automatically remember what I learned and defend myself. Why is this? Was I not taught well? Did I not retain what I learned well? No, it is not even close to any of those things. The real answer to the questions is that my mind was never programmed in the first place. Sure, I was learning the techniques and using them night in and night out, but the key word here is "learning." I was programming my mind for self-defense. It was not programmed yet. To truly program my mind to react the same way every time depending on the situation, I would have had to spend more time and would have had to practice even though I was no longer going to classes. I stopped practicing the techniques I learned in tae kwon do, and now I do not know them any longer.

That is what martial art is about. It is a lifestyle. Self-defense, respect, calmness in stressful situations, healthy body and mind are all what martial art teaches. Mr. Yoon was in his fifties at the time of my training with him, and he had been involved in martial art his entire life. He was an eight-time black belt. Maybe he is a nine-time black belt now. I do not know. He is a chief master in tae kwon do. I guarantee if you tried to attack Chief Master Yoon, he would not have to think to defend himself. That is the power of martial art. It is programming your mind to react in any situation of self-defense without thinking about it. It is moving the techniques, the kicks, the strikes, the throws, and the philosophies from your conscious mind to your subconscious mind. It is that simple. What is not simple is the consistency in which you do this and doing it for a lifetime. The same applies for being positive.

You will have to practice being positive over and over and over. You will have to practice it for a lifetime to become like Mr. Yoon in his art. If you practice being positive for a year and then stop, begin allowing yourself to think negative thoughts and fears, start hanging out with negative people, and do not make a conscious effort until your subconscious is reprogrammed, you will not truly be a positive person. I am not truly a tae kwon do green belt any longer because I do not practice tae kwon do every week. I may be able to say I am a green belt, but I could not use any of the techniques I learned nine years ago if someone was to attack me. But when someone attacks me with negativity, I do not have to think. I simply react as Chief Master Yoon would react if someone attacked him physically. No matter what negativity comes at me and no matter from whom and which direction, I can disarm it and overcome the attack. It is like a karate movie for me. If ten people were to attack me with negativity at the same time, I could fend them off simultaneously and overcome their attack, submitting them into positivity. I have studied the power of positivity my entire life. I have practiced it far more than Mr. Yoon has practiced tae kwon do. I practice being positive twenty-four hours a day, seven days a week.

This is the true power of positivity. I do not know how much longer it would have taken me to have programmed my subconscious in tae kwon do to automatically defend myself if I were to be attacked, but if I would have, there would have been many other things besides self-defense that would have been programmed, wouldn't there? Martial art may be self-defense, but when programmed into the subconscious, it becomes much more. It becomes a lifestyle of confidence, respect, and much more. Positivity, when programmed into your subconscious, will become true happiness, success, health, better relationships and much more. That is the power of positivity.

There is one more thing that will come out of you being a truly positive person. I will talk about this in more detail in later chapters, but there is always energy inside of us and all around us. There is energy on earth that is always moving around us. There is energy from other people that we come in contact with and tap into. Some call this chemistry, which it is. But it is also their energy. We also can, from time to time, read one another's minds and feel other people's energy. We have all done it. Our brains produce energy. Our bodies produce energy. That is why we must eat and sleep to restore our energy. When you think positive thoughts all the time, you will be putting off positive energy. Your body will be running off positive energy. Your batteries will be charged all the time. Other people will tap into your positive energy. Positive people will feel your positive energy. Positive energy is like a magnet. It attracts good things. This is the same with negative energy. It attracts bad things. Good and evil, remember? Now let's expand good and evil to positive and negative. It is real. You will learn more about how positive energy works later, but for now just know that positive energy is also something that will come from the power of positivity.

Now it is time to put down the book again. Get the piece of paper that you look at every night and day. Write this exactly.

I am a positive person. I always think positive thoughts and say positive things. When I make decisions, I look at them in a positive manner and make positive decisions. I look at obstacles and challenges through positive eyes. When opportunities arise, I will see them because I am a positive person. Everything I do each day will be a positive thing. When I write to others, I will write in a positive manner. I am a confident person. I will smile often and will smile at others while I talk to them. I will smile with my eyes. I will stand up straight when I walk, with my shoulders back. I will look and feel confident when I walk. When I am around others, they will know that I am a positive person, and they will be drawn to my positivity. My relationships will be better because of my positivity, and my family life will be better because of it also. I am going to become the most positive person I know. My positive attitude will bring me more energy, and I will feel fantastic physically because I am now a positive person. I am my own best friend. I like myself, and I am a great person.

CHAPTER 4

What You Should Be Saying
When You Talk to Yourself

What should you be saying when you talk to yourself? Put the book down and think about that for a moment. You now know the answer, but it will go deep in your subconscious if you put the book down and think about it before you start reading this chapter. The techniques in this chapter are the most important thing to know so take a moment and think about it before you begin.

Now let me tell you what you should be saying when you talk to yourself. I use the word "saying," but I really mean "thinking" more than "saying." However, we do talk to ourselves all the time, don't we? I often find myself talking to myself. Sometimes people make fun of me, and I just turn to them and say with a big smile on my face, "Talking to yourself is a sign of high intelligence." Did you know that? It is a fact. I know that because I talk to myself, I am not smarter than anyone else, but do not underestimate the power of talking to yourself. Now if you talk to yourself with other people around you constantly and do not listen to other people when they talk, you might want to go see a doctor. Seriously though, talking to yourself is very common. If you find yourself talking to yourself, do not stop. It is good to talk to yourself. I am going to talk a lot more in this chapter about what you should be thinking more though, because we are always thinking when we are not talking, aren't we?

As you become more of a positive person, you will find that you will become more comfortable with yourself. You should be your own best friend. If you are not your own best friend, then you must start becoming your own best friend right now. Think about it. You are with yourself all day, every day. You never get a break from yourself. You better spend the rest of your life liking yourself. I learned this in my late twenties. It is mind-boggling how many people do not like themselves. I like myself so much it makes me sick. I like myself more and more all the time. I do not mean this to sound cocky, and I do not think I am better than anyone, but I want you to know that I know how it feels to truly like oneself. It is not because I think I am that great or better than anyone else, because I am not. It is just because I like myself. I like who I am inside. I like who I have become and where I am headed in life. Do you? If not, then it's time to change this immediately. It starts right now. Know that one second after you decide that you are going to start liking yourself it begins. It's that simple.

When I was in my late twenties, I realized that I was all I had. I was single for almost two years, and I spent a lot of time by myself. I had dated on and off for that two years, but I would not let myself get into a serious relationship. I was enjoying being by myself, living by myself, pretty much going through life by myself. It was the first time since I was in my early twenties that I was truly on my own and I decided to explore it. After about six months, I started to really enjoy being alone. It was weird at first. I did not know what to think and how to act. Then it suddenly kicked in. I cooked dinner for myself, watched TV, watched movies by myself, went to sleep by myself, worked, and hung out with friends when I wanted to. It became very pleasant. It was in those two years that I learned to like myself. I was already a very positive person by then because I had read many books, been to many seminars, and listened to many tapes on positive thinking and self-help. I had positive energy flowing through my veins. You might say, "Well, that is why you were so happy by yourself." And I would say, "You are right." It played a big factor in the equation, but I had to learn how to like being with myself alone also in those two years. I had to learn how to talk to myself and what thoughts to think while I was alone often. Being alone for six months or a year is one thing, but being alone for two years was something else. It gave me time to do some soul-searching. You do not have to spend two years alone to achieve liking yourself though. No matter what your circumstances are you will spend much time alone and learn to truly like yourself.

What I realized during those two years was that I could have inner peace with myself. I also realized that I could become my own friend as an adult. Do you remember when you were very young? Did you have make-believe friends? Did you talk to yourself a lot? Observe young children, children five, six, seven years old. Watch them when they are playing alone. You can do it at a friend's house or anywhere. If you have children, you know what I am talking about. Young children are usually content with themselves, aren't they? They can sit and play with a toy and talk to themselves for hours. We learn to be our own best friend when we are children, but as we become adults, we do this less because society does not want people to be seen talking to themselves and sitting by themselves in a room with other people and having a big smile on their face for no reason and talking to themselves. We make fun of people that do this and think they are strange. But are they?

Then there are those people that truly just do not like themselves. Here is why. When you tell yourself that you do not like yourself, you are not going to. It is that subconscious thing going on again. Even when people think to themselves that they are ugly, fat, short, that they have an ugly nose, small hands, weird feet, that they talk funny, are not very smart, are not social, and so on, they are being negative. Negative thoughts will produce a negative you. Write that down. "Negative thoughts will produce a negative me." For some reason, as we grow older from those young children that are best friends with themselves, we stop doing that. It is time to start doing that again. That's what I learned in those two years being by myself. I now practice it no matter who I am with. It is time for you to become your own best friend again. Have you ever had a friend that you called your best friend? Have you ever had a friend that you felt completely comfortable with? You can say anything around them and laugh and smile. Conversations are effortless. You feel truly happy around them. That is how you need to become with yourself. When you are by yourself, you should feel that with you. You should be your own best friend. Here is how you do it.

First, you must always think positive thoughts. When you are alone and you spend time by yourself, pay attention to how you are thinking to yourself. Pay attention to what you are saying in your head. When the conversation you are having with yourself starts to turn negative, stop it. This is hard at first. What you are going to probably have to do is stop the conversation completely with yourself and start it over. Just stop thinking about what you were thinking about when it turned negative and start over. Practice this often. Tell yourself right now that you are not going to have negative conversations and thoughts with yourself from this day forward. Say it! Say it out loud. Put the book down and take a minute to be by yourself. Tell yourself that you are going to start liking yourself, become your best friend, and not have negative conversations with yourself any longer. Tell yourself that you are going to learn how to like yourself better than anyone else in the world, more than your girlfriend or boyfriend, wife or husband, more than your family, your friends and more than your children. If you do this, you will treat those people much better. You know this. If you do not like yourself, how can you like others? If you don't treat yourself right how can you treat others the right way? Now if you like yourself better than anyone else in the world, how much will you like others? How much happier will you be around others? How much of a better time will you have with others? How much better will your life be? How much better will you make people around you feel? How exciting it is for you that today is going to be the day you truly start liking yourself.

When you have positive conversations with yourself, everything good comes from it. It is the same as being a positive person all the time, but now I am talking specifically about when you are alone and when you are thinking by yourself. I am talking about when you are all alone in a room, driving your car by yourself, or at your office alone. I am talking about when you are having a conversation about your life to yourself, about how you think your life is going. I am talking about those times when you are reflecting on everything you have and the things you want, about what you have achieved, how you eat, and how you raise your children. From this day forward, it is time to practice having positive conversations about those things with yourself. This is much different than when you are with a friend or group of people and they are talking negative. It is different than when you are at work around negative people. This is between you and yourself. It is what you are saying to yourself.

Do you talk positively to yourself? Do you smile when you think to yourself? Do you feel good when you are alone thinking to yourself? When you look at yourself in the mirror do you like what you see? It is OK if the answer is "no." Everyone has negative conversations with themselves. I have negative conversations with myself. There are times still that I must make a conscious effort to be positive when I am talking to myself. Remember, no one is perfect, and this is a life journey. It is a marathon, not a sprint. But it is easy and fun and can start immediately if you choose. You are going to have to make a conscious effort to talk positive to yourself. It may not happen overnight. The good news is that you will have a lot of time to practice this technique of positive thinking, won't you? You are stuck with yourself. I want you to ask yourself this question, "When I lie on my deathbed, what will I think about my life?" Will you have regrets? Will you feel you did not live life to the fullest? Let me share a secret with you? Living life to the fullest is not driving an expensive car, living in a huge house, and having a lot of money. Those things are all nice to have, but living life to the fullest is being truly happy. Are you truly happy? Living life to the fullest is being truly happy with yourself. If you are truly happy with yourself. If you are your own best friend, you have achieved the most important thing in life there is to achieve. Everything else will come after this one achievement. It is above everything because without you being happy and fulfilled with yourself, you can not completely ever be happy and fulfilled with every other aspect of your life. Begin to observe what I am talking about and you understand that I am right. You will understand exactly what I am talking about.

When you become truly happy with yourself through positive conversations with yourself, you will then begin to understand what happiness is. You will make others around you happy. People always tell me, "You are happy all the time." I may know someone for six months or a year, and then one day at a party or at my office they come out of nowhere and say it. I love to hear it when someone comes out of nowhere and tells me that. I know that they have been observing me and that I am helping them to be more positive, even if I only see them every so often. The reason I am happy all the time is because I have positive conversations with myself and I like myself. It is not because of the car I drive or the house I live in or how much money I have in the bank. That means nothing. It is because when I sit by myself, I have happy, positive conversations with myself. This makes me a happy person. I have true happiness.

When I was a teenager and drove a fifteen-year-old stick shift Toyota Corolla and worked at a fast-food restaurant making hamburgers and did not have a penny to my name, I was happy all the time. Does life throw challenges at me? You better believe it! Do I get down sometimes? Absolutely! But I have learned that if I always tell myself things are going to be all right and mean it, they are. This is something you must learn. When bad things happen to you, you must tell yourself repeatedly that it is going to be all right and mean it. Do not dwell on bad things. Do not talk to yourself about bad things.

If you notice, I am talking a lot about you making a conscious effort to like yourself and to have positive conversations with yourself. That is because if you are going to reprogram yourself to like yourself, and most of the time be having positive conversations with yourself, you will be automatically programming your subconscious. This programming will happen faster because you are always talking to yourself. From the minute you wake up until the minute you fall asleep, you are thinking to yourself. Even your dreams can be positive or negative. All you have to do is make a conscious effort to think positive thoughts, and the programming will happen naturally in your subconscious. You are going to spend the rest of your life with yourself. Friends are going to come and go. Jobs are going to come and go. Even relationships are going to come and go. Your children will be on their own someday. But you are the constant in your life. You are all you really have. You must make a conscious effort to have happy, positive conversations with yourself and to truly like yourself in order to become a positive person. Once you program yourself to have positive conversations you know it. You will see that you no longer have to consciously think about it. It will be happening naturally. Once this happens you will start to see things in your head and out of your eyes that you have never seen before. Things will start to look different. The sky will look different. Your house will look different. You will look at people differently. Basically, the world around you will become a different place. A better place. You will feel a sense of wellbeing. You will like the things you do just a little better. Everything all day from the minute you wake up until the time you go to sleep will be a little better. It's that fantastic. It's like waking up and being in utopia. You will know that world is the same place, but your world will be different. You will understand that your world and the outside world are two different places that live inside of you simultaneously and once mastered properly with a positive attitude become two places that are one in perfect harmony.

Observe people that are sitting by themselves when you are in public places and they do not know that you are looking at them. Watch someone that is by themselves and is not doing anything. Not reading, not looking at a computer, but just sitting by themselves, staring into the air. Watch their eyes, their cheeks, their lips, and the muscles in their face. See if they are frowning a little bit or if their lips are just slightly turned up. See if their eyes look sad, mad, or happy. They will be simply sitting by themselves, doing nothing, but you will be amazed at how much you can tell about them by just watching their face. You will see what kind of conversation they are having with themselves. You will see if they look at peace or stressed out. You will see a big difference in the people that have positive conversations with themselves and the ones that do not. You will see the difference. You can be in line in the grocery store. It can be anywhere. Just start looking around you. Watch people in your office or at work while they are working. This will help you realize that there is a difference in people that have positive conversations with themselves. You will see it on their faces. You will see it in their body language, how they sit, how they hold their arms. Everything about them will be different, depending on how they are thinking to themselves. Then watch how they talk if someone approaches them or if they must talk for some reason. Listen to the tone of their voice. Watch their body language. How they engage with others. How they look at others. Observe how their facial expression appears. Listen to the words they speak and the conversation they engage in. Listen to what they talk about and how they speak about the subject and see if you they were a positive self-thinker or a negative self-thinker.

How do you practice becoming your own best friend? You do it when you are alone. What if you are never alone? What if you wake up, get the kids ready for school, then drive them to school, then go to work and talk for a living, then pick the kids up from school, cook dinner, and get the kids ready for bed every day? No problem. What you are going to have to do is make some time for yourself to be alone. How great is it that you are going to make some time for you and that you are going to sit quietly alone and have a positive, happy conversation with yourself? It just sounds good, doesn't it? It is good. The good news for doing this is that you are with yourself every day and every night. You even sleep with yourself every night. You have the rest of your life to make a little extra time for you to be alone and to have a pleasant, positive conversation with yourself. Just make some time. You are not going anywhere. Do not be hard on yourself and stress out over making time for yourself. Just do a little at a time. You will see how much you like it and how much better you feel. This will make you naturally want to make more time to be by yourself.

What about when you are not by yourself? What about when times are completely hectic and crazy? What about when you are stressed out and having a bad day? What about when something bad happens to you? This is the time to really have a positive conversation with yourself. Once your subconscious is reprogrammed, you will not have to consciously think about thinking positive thoughts when you are going through tough times and having tough days. But at first, you will have to make a conscious effort to have positive conversations with yourself when things are not going as you would like. This will make things go as you would like. When bad things are happening around you or to you and you think to yourself, tell yourself that it is going to be OK and that you are going to be fine and believe it. Tell yourself that you are going to stay positive and happy even though things are not going well. Tell yourself that you are secure with the situation because you have yourself, and that is all you need to get through tough times because you can accomplish and overcome anything. Tell yourself you are a positive person, and you will find solutions to problems and make bad situations good. You can do it. That is what truly happy and positive people do. Truly happy and positive people have problems all the time, but they look at challenges and obstacles as speed bumps, not unscalable brick walls. The look at bad situations as something they will conquer and will make them stronger. Truly happy people look at bad situations and immediately start figuring out how to turn them around. Everyone has bad times. It is how we handle them that makes the difference.

When you are faced with an obstacle or are having a bad day, think to yourself, "This is going to be all right. Everything is going to be OK." It is that simple. You just must keep saying it to yourself repeatedly until you believe it. And then guess what happens? Your subconscious will start figuring out how to make the situation better. It will help guide you to see things clearly and make the correct decisions or think the correct thoughts to make the bad situation into a good one, because your subconscious is a positive subconscious and has been programmed to make bad situations into good situations through positive thinking. That is what truly happy and positive people do. They believe that everything will be all right. They do not doubt that it will be all right. They know without a shadow of a doubt that it will be all right, and if they do have doubts, they overcome them.

The most important thing that you can do if something bad happens to you is to think to yourself, "What is the worst thing that can happen here?" Face the worst thing that a bad situation can throw at you or the worst outcome that can come about. Once you think about it to yourself, you have faced the worst of any situation, haven't you? Once you face the worst of what a situation can throw at you or the worst outcome a situation can become, you no longer fear it because you have faced it. Then all you have to do is start thinking positive thoughts to make things better. Tell yourself that it does not matter how long it takes to make a bad situation into a good one, but you are going to do it. This will take practice, but once you do this for the first time, you will never look back. Once you turn a bad situation into a good one because you truly believed in yourself and think positive thoughts through it, you have the secret of how not to be negative through bad times. When you do this, it will help you think positive and happy thoughts all the time. But when things are going well and you are alone, you will then experience the power of thinking positive thoughts and having positive conversations with yourself. All of this together will program your subconscious to keep you calm in stressful situations and to see the positive in all situations. You will then maintain a positive attitude in stressful situations and when bad things happen, as well as have positive conversations and thoughts with yourself about these situations. Do you see how much power you will have over bad situations? Every bad and stressful situation and unexpected happening becomes just something else you are going to overcome and sleigh with your positive self-talk, your positive verbal talk, your positive actions, and your positive attitude overall. Everyone around you will know that you are going to handle all stressful and negative situations with no fear and knowing that they cannot shake you or get you down. They will know that you are a problem solver and see the positive in every situation. That is the true definition of a, "Positive Attitude".

There is another way that you must learn to think to yourself. You must tell yourself that everything is going to be OK because God is with you and will lead you in the right directions. When you do this and believe it, you will feel a sense of well-being that is indescribable.

The reason you will feel this is because God will be there for you. You do not have to think very hard about this. You only have to say to yourself, "God, lead me in the right directions to have the things that I want in life, and show me how to be a happy, positive person." That is all you have to say to yourself. No matter what believe about God or a higher power know that God for the purposes of this book is the higher power that you draw from and know exists in the universe and on a higher level. Do not go on and on in your head to yourself about the things you want and why you want them. Your subconscious already knows what you want. You think about it all the time. Just ask God to guide you, and then let go mentally. Do not think to yourself anymore. Take a moment to clear your head and just relax. Take a deep breath. Then go about what you were doing. I like to do this when I am driving, but I can do it when I am at my office, in my house alone, or even when I am with a group of people. I can do it anytime, anywhere. It is just part of me talking to myself. Make this a part of talking to yourself, and you will have the things you want in life and live a happy, positive life. Instead of talking to god, practice on receiving God. Practice opening up to the feelings that will come when you receive God.

When you think to yourself about your life, do you say nice things about yourself and the life you live? Do you like your life? Try this next time you think about your life and what you have accomplished so far. Think about all the good things that you have done with your life. Think about the good times you have had and the people that you have had them with. When you think about what you have not accomplished that you would like to, tell yourself that you are going to have all the things in life you wish someday. When you think positive thoughts and about positive things, you feel good.

You can smile with your brain. Try it sometime when you have your eyes closed and are lying in the dark in bed. Do not smile with your mouth. Keep your mouth straight, but instead, smile with your brain. You will feel the smile. This is the positive chemicals that you will learn to release inside of you without having to make physical action. Once you learn how to do this and think about your life at the same time, you will feel a sense of happiness you have never felt.

Once you do this, you will learn how to feel positive while lying by yourself in the dark. When negative thoughts come over you while you are lying in bed in the dark, you will be able to control them easier.

Now when you are talking to yourself and thinking to yourself and you put all these techniques together, what do you think will happen? There are not many ways to think or speak negative thoughts to yourself, are there? We have covered what to do while you are with other people, by yourself, and even while lying in bed in the dark by yourself. We have covered how to become your own best friend. Now we must talk about how to use all this all the time. When you wake up every day, what do you do? Usually you either jump out of bed or hit your snooze button and go back to sleep. You also begin thinking about things from the minute you wake up. Even if you do go back to sleep and hit snooze, you will have to eventually wake up and get out of the bed. After you do get out of bed, no matter how you do it, you will start thinking immediately to yourself. What you start thinking about will set your day. It will make your morning a good one or a bad one. Once you figure this out, you will look at life out of different eyes, as we already established.

What is perspective? The definition of perspective is "a view or vista," "a mental view or outlook," "the relationship of aspects of a subject to each other and to a whole," "subject evaluation of relative significance, a point of view," "the ability to perceive things in their actual interrelations or comparative importance." In other words, perspective is what we make of it. How you perceive the world, your life, the people around you, and yourself is what your world becomes. The reason we do not think about this is because it has become a subconscious function. By thinking and acting the way we do day in and day out, our perspective of our lives and the world becomes our world. It becomes our reality. Because we do this for years at a time, it can happen subtly, without us knowing it. But now you do know it. That is what the successful, happy people know. They understand perspective.

Why do we have a saying "People change"? It is because people do change. Look back at your life. You are basically the same person, but you have changed over the years. It is not just because you are getting older. Have you ever seen people that have said "I have not changed a bit at all in my lifetime" and they are older people? Or have you ever talked to people that have done many different things, been to different places, experienced many things, and changed substantially since they were a younger person and say they are a totally different person then when they were younger? That is all because they have either kept their thinking the same or they changed their thinking, which made them change as a person. They decided to stay the same or to become different people than they were by trying new things and experiences.

If you look at your life, you have probably had sometimes that you have made some major changes. Sometimes we are forced to do this, but most times we do it because we decide to. Before you made changes, you probably thought about them a lot and for a long time. But those are the changes that you can think of right away. Have you ever changed in your life and you do not really know why? Are you the same exact person that you were five, ten, fifteen, twenty years ago? Maybe your career has dictated some of this, or maybe relationships have. And maybe you have. Or there could have been things that happened in your life that forced these changes. It is probably a combination of all this, but the bottom line is that you have changed and are not the same person that you were years ago.

As life passes by, you are going to change more times. Now it is time to change how you want to. Now you know the secret to change. You will change either way most likely. Why not change the way you would like to change the next time? Why not help your partner change the way they would like to? What if you and your partner could change together as a unit and as individuals? Isn't this the ultimate achievement? The athletes, movie stars, businesspeople, and generally happy people we have been talking about are practicing this. They are constantly becoming who they want to become through their thinking and their actions. I can tell you this because I have talked to these people, read their books, seen them speak at seminars, and more. I pay attention to things like this. And most importantly, I have been doing this my entire life. I know that when I want to do something or change in a certain way, all I have to do is start thinking about it all the time. If I think about something repeatedly, I know I am going to do it. If I do not want to do something that I am thinking repeatedly, I just stop thinking about it and go on to something else. I just change my perspective.

Our perspective is what we make it. You must learn that your perspective of your life is what your life will become. Now it is time to start learning how to make a perspective of your life and then how to achieve that perspective. Do you know why most people do not achieve what they perceive what they would like their life to become? It is because they give up on their perspective. Why do they do this? Because they have programmed themselves to quit because they are not good enough to do it what it takes to make their perspective reality. They do not give it enough time to go from their conscious to their subconscious. Why is this? It is because, firstly, they do not know that their subconscious can even be programmed and how important it is to program their subconscious correctly, and secondly, they have never had the experience of their subconscious being programmed on a conscious level. Now you know that this can happen and does exist, but you must experience it yourself to really believe it. You must live it to know it and then practice it to master it. What I am talking about will take time to master. Most people that know this have spent their life doing it. I am not trying to say that it will take a lifetime to learn this. It is already happening now and now you have the secret to all of it. You now know it is simple and fun once you know how to do. You will have to be patient and persistent with this knowledge though. But you will see that once you start and are persistent, time goes by very fast while changing and creating your perspective. Life seems to pass by fast, doesn't it? You will have to practice, practice, practice. You can speed up this process dramatically by reading more books like this, listening to CDs on things like this, watching positive attitude shows, attending seminars about positive thinking and changing your life. They are in your city, and the books and shows are everywhere. Once you become consistent with doing different things to learn how to change your perspective, the process will speed up. It that easy. I will say it repeatedly in this book. You are going to have to keep at this and believe it will happen to you. You are going to have to hear this from other people's perspectives, which will help you learn more techniques. You will be able to relate better to other people's perspectives from a book or seminar that you attend over others. Do this part-time, but be consistent at it. Make it part of your goals.

Now put the book down again. Close your eyes and tell yourself that you are going to change your perspective. Say it to yourself until you believe it. You are not going to stress yourself out over it, but you are going to be consistent. Put the book down.

Now write this down. Put it on the piece of paper that you look at every day, the one that you recite at night before you go to bed and in the morning. Make it part of your life. That is what the successful people do every day and night. They are not lucky. We would like to think that they are, but they are not. I could give a negative thinker that does not know how to be successful $2 million tomorrow, and they would lose it all within a year. That is how this works. I can give a positive person that knows how to be successful and has lost everything because they took a risk and lost $5,000, and they will turn it into $2 million in one year. See the difference? It is perspective of money, success, happiness, themselves and much more. "What you think, you will achieve." Good or bad. If you think you are unlucky, unhappy, undeserving, then that is what you will become. If you think you are lucky, happy, and deserving, you will become that. It is that easy. It takes believing it can and will happen, not just hoping that it will happen. It takes seeing it happen to you one time. It takes doing it. It also takes observing other people that are doing it and learning from them. You must become a professional positive thinker, just like the successful people who become professional actors, professional athletes, professional businesspeople, etc. They practice what they want to become repeatedly. They also stay positive and tell themselves that they are going to be the best at what they do.

What about people that you would consider a professional parent? How about someone that you would consider being a professional housewife or husband. What about if you want to be a professional "relaxer" and not do anything? It does not matter. What matters is what you want. What only matters are what you want out of life. It is your life, and we are all different. Remember this: the world is made up of all different people with different perspectives. We are all different. The world needs all perspectives in it, and that is what makes the world what it is for human beings. Do not become someone that you want to be because you think others will accept you for it. Become who you want to be, and others will have no choice but to accept you because they will see that you are truly happy.

It does not matter how old or young you are. Never ever use age as an excuse. Using age as an excuse is one of the worst kinds of negative thinking you can have. Saying to yourself "I am too young to do this" or "I am too old to do this" is crazy thinking. I hear it all the time. I see it in people's eyes and on their faces when I talk to them. You are never too old or too young to change your perspective and your thinking to positive. Put the book down again and tell yourself that. Go ahead, put it down. Close your eyes and tell yourself that you are never too young or old to become a positive person. Then write it down on your piece of paper. Do it now.

The last way that you are going to have to learn to reprogram your subconscious and think to yourself is that you always must find the good in everything. This may sound cliché but vital to having true success in achieving a positive attitude. Every day things happen to us, good and bad. We are constantly making decisions and completing tasks repeatedly, all day long. We are achieving mini goals, large-scale goals, and completing tasks all our waking hours. Even while we sleep, we are completing a task. We are letting our bodies rest and rejuvenate. When you are moving throughout your day, you need to understand that you must always find the good in everything. When you are talking to yourself, you always must find the good in everything. Once you pay attention to what I am saying, you will see that there is good and bad in every situation. The world revolves around creating problems and then fixing them. What do you do at your job every day? The chances are you are always fixing some kind of problem, no matter what your occupation is. And if you are not directly fixing problems, then the chances are problems will arise in your department that must be fixed. This is the nature of the world. This is because, as I said earlier, the world is not a perfect place.

When you go home every day from work, what are you faced with? Everyone has challenges to deal with—children, spouses, health, money, and so on. We must overcome our challenges constantly. There is a secret that successful, happy positive people know about challenges. They practice this secret all the time. The secret is that when they have obstacles and challenges, they always look at the good things in them. They find the positive in them. They decide they are not going to dwell on the negative aspects of problems and obstacles. That is what I do every day. That is what you are going to learn how to do every day.

So how do we teach ourselves to always look at the positive in everything? Get your piece of paper out again. The one you look at every morning, all day, and at night before bed. Write down "Challenges get me up." That is, it. Challenges need to get you up, not down. When you have obstacles, challenges, and problems, you need to get up for them. You do that by thinking to yourself, "What are the good points of this challenge, obstacle, or problem? What are the positive points?"

Sometimes it will seem that there are no positive points to something that happens to you. Sometimes very bad things happen to us, don't they? Know now that bad things happen to everyone. No one is safe or exempt from bad things happening to them. And the more things and ventures you embark on the more problems you will encounter. The key is to minimize bad things happening to you and then to work through bad things with a positive attitude by finding the good in every situation. When you think to yourself about a bad situation or something bad that is happening to you, first find the good points and then dwell on them. If you cannot find anything good or positive in a situation, keep telling yourself that eventually something will come about that is positive. Just keep saying to yourself, "There has to be something positive in this situation." Eventually, you will find something positive. The more your subconscious gets programmed to be a positive subconscious, the faster you will find good in every bad situation. Once you find the good aspects of a bad situation, you must dwell only on the good aspects. You must think of the good aspects repeatedly. You must tell yourself that it is going to be all right. Then when you think about the negative and bad aspects of a bad situation, you must think about them in a problem-solving way, not a hopeless, negative way. Challenges get you up, remember? This is very important for you to believe. When you look at your list every day, make sure that you think or say "Challenges get me up" in a loud, happy, positive tone.

Once you program your mind to find the good in every situation, you will see how much different your life becomes. You will see how easy it is to make people around you think that their problems are not so bad. When you have conversations with people and they talk about their bad, negative problems and you find a good, positive aspect of their problem, they will feel better and maybe find a solution to their problem. This is a very important technique to learn because problems are always going to arise in life. There is always going to be something to deal with until the day we die. I look at this as a happy thing. I am smiling right now thinking about how wonderful of a place the world is and how challenges get me up. I know that the more I can overcome challenges, the more I can challenge myself and the better I will become. The more you challenge yourself, the better you will become.

How do athletes become professionals? How does a singer get on the radio? How do great parents have wonderful children? They are always challenging themselves. They are constantly pushing themselves, which makes them "elite," "professional." When you think to yourself about a problem or a bad situation, look for the good in it, and then dwell on the good in it until it goes away. Do not dwell on the negative aspects of a problem. Instead, dwell on finding solutions to the problem. Dwell on telling yourself that you are going to fix the problem and that challenges get you up. That is how you think to yourself. That is how you should be going through life. If you are not, then it is time to start. Tell yourself that you are going to find the good in every bad situation, and then dwell on the good aspects while overcoming and fixing the bad aspects.

When I encounter problems, I always know that something good is going to come out of it. It is so strange and so hard to explain in a book how it feels to know that something good is going to come out of a bad situation every time something bad happens. I just keep thinking to myself that things are going to be all right. I keep dwelling on the good I can find and the good that arises. As I solve my problems, I then have better and positive things to dwell on, so something that started as only a problem becomes a distant problem. I move away from the problem in my brain while moving toward the positive things that are arising from the problem. There have been times in my life that I have had very bad things happen to me, only to discover that something very good came out of it years later. Maybe I learned a valuable lesson that kept me from having something much worse happen to me in the future. That has happened to me. Take the time to practice these techniques and it will happen to you. Once you realize how easy it is to not dwell on the negative in a bad situation you will never do it again. Once you realize how rewarding it can be to see the positive in every bad situation you will learn one of the most important techniques of all. Why, because bad things and bad situations are going to always be part of your life. It is part of being human. What does not have to be part of being human is the way you handle them. Take special notice of your thoughts now as you enter and encounter negative situations. Help others to see the positive in negative situations. Become a leader in negative situations. Strive to have a truly positive attitude.

CHAPTER 5

Exercise and Diet

"Motivation is what gets you started; habit is what keeps you going." Why does exercise belong in a positive-thinking book? Exercise is a physical thing, not a mental thing. Most people do not realize how important it is to exercise and how exercise affects your mental attitude. Think of your body as a machine for a moment. Machines have moving parts, and they require maintenance to keep in peak performance. Our bodies are a machine, aren't they? We move our arms, our legs. We walk, talk, see, hold things, and perform many other physical functions all day long. When we sleep, our bodies go to work repairing and maintaining our bodies and mind. Our machine (our bodies) never really stops. Our machine truly stops the day we die.

Think for a second about a hypothetical person that thinks positive thoughts all the time and is so unhealthy that they have diabetes, high blood pressure, and other diseases. Now think about a hypothetical person that is in perfect physical condition but always thinks negative thoughts and never achieves anything they want in life. Is either of these people truly a positive person? Are they a positive being? No, they are not. To truly achieve a total state of positiveness, you must exercise. Exercise is a vital part of life. Maybe you are saying to yourself right now, "I have never exercised a day in my life, and I am not going to start now." Do not worry. Do not get stressed out. If you do not become an exercise freak in the next year or two, you are going to be fine and still be able to achieve all that you want in life through a positive attitude.

What I am talking about is just doing something. Not completely changing your life. You have spent a lifetime up until now to be who you are. But you are reading this book because you obviously want more. I am talking about starting to exercise the same way I spoke about becoming a truly positive person. It starts gradually. But the key is consistency. This is a marathon, not a sprint. What I am talking about is just doing something every day, at least five days a week. That is the goal. It does not have to start this way, but this is the goal. You can start by doing something once per week, and then work up from there. Now it is time to put the book down again and write on your piece of paper that you read every day. Write down that you are going to start exercising at least once per week and that you are going to gradually work out more until one day you are exercising at least five days per week. If you exercise at least five days per week now, then write down that exercise is one of the key components to living a positive life and that you are never going to stop exercising.

I am fortunate because I have always exercised. I have never, since the day I graduated high school, not been a member of a gym. And I have not taken much time off from going to the gym. Just recently, I have incorporated jogging into exercise again, and it is amazing. You may think to yourself, "OK, so you have always exercised, and you have always thought positive thoughts. Lucky you. No wonder you are writing this book." I cannot tell you how hard it is sometimes to go to the gym, how hard it is to get in the car and drive there, then get out of the car and work out. Or to go for a walk or a jog. Sometimes I would rather be doing anything but working out. Once I begin though, and after I am done, I always say to myself, "I am so glad I did it." Being athletic and working out all my life is like a good curse. My body knows the difference when I do not exercise, and it does not like it. My brain knows the difference when I do not work out, and it does not like it. I am forced to work out for the rest of my life. I have been programmed by my subconscious that I must work out to feel right. I have done this by saying to myself all my life that if I do not work out, I do not feel right, and I feel guilty. I have told other people that I must work out to feel right my entire life, which has assured my subconscious that I must work out to feel right, both physically and mentally. Now it is time for you to start programming your mind into thinking that you must exercise to feel right.

If you have a job that keeps you active, like moving furniture, lifting things, walking all day, standing all day, or doing any type of physical activity all day, then you are already exercising every day. You are halfway there. You still need to be doing some form of exercise other than work, but you are doing something five days a week. But you should be on an exercise schedule that is geared toward health also. If you go to an office and sit all day then you are going to have to exercise to feel at your optimal, positive self. This is the same as when I described how you are going to become positive and reprogram your mind. You must start by not beating yourself up over it. You must tell yourself that you are just going to make a change, and it starts today.

What does exercise do for your body and mind? Our bodies are not meant to sit down all day and night, eat bad food, think bad thoughts, and be unhealthy. That is not what we are on earth for. Maybe you are saying to yourself, "But I like eating bad foods and thinking the way I think." I say to you, liking yourself is a very important part of life, but if you like yourself now, imagine how much more you will like yourself if you exercise and think positive thoughts all the time. This is what exercise does for your body and mind. Our bodies and our minds are connected. Our brains connect to our spinal cords for a reason. Our brains send chemical signals to our spinal cords for a reason. We always have many chemical reactions going on. When we exercise, our bodies work at an optimal level, which helps our brains to function at an optimal level. When we think positive thoughts all the time, it helps our bodies to function at an optimal level. When we function at an optimal level, we then live an optimal life.

Our bodies also have hormones in them and produce hormones by different kinds of methods. When you exercise and then eat the right kinds of foods, it will help your body's hormones to stay at normal levels. The definition of a hormone is "a chemical substance produced in the body that controls or regulates the activity of certain cells or organs. Many hormones are secreted by special glands, such as thyroid hormone produced by the thyroid gland. Hormones are essential for every activity of life, including the process of digestion, metabolism, growth, reproduction, and mood control. Many hormones such as neurotransmitters, are active in more than one physical process." When you are eating right, exercising, and thinking right, it is safe to say that you will be feeling right, isn't it? When your hormones are at normal levels for your body and not too high or too low, it will help you think positive thoughts and be a positive person all the time. Exercise will help do this and will help every aspect of your life.

Diet is a large part of exercise as well. We will talk more about diet later, but always remember that "you are what you eat." The saying is so true. And you are what you drink. And you are what you think. Now if you eat right, drink right, exercise, and think right, who are you going to become? You are going to become a pretty awesome person. I have news for you. You are a pretty awesome person now. You are just going to improve your life and take yourself physically and mentally to a level that most people only dream of. It is right in front of you now. All you have to do is go get it! You are now behind the curtain and know what people that have what you want are doing.

What kind of exercising should you be doing? Should you go join a gym tomorrow? Should you go out and buy some running shoes or a bicycle or a jump rope? There are many ways you can exercise. I am going to tell you what I believe to be the best forms of exercise for a positive attitude, but there are no bad exercises except for an exercise that will hurt you. It is very important to start slowly if you do not exercise. You will get stronger and have more stamina as time goes by. Starting slowly is very smart, and there is nothing wrong with doing what you can. Listen to your body, and do not over exercise. Over exercising is bad for you also. I am guilty of over exercising at times. I believe that walking and jogging are by far the most important exercise you can do to have a positive attitude. When you walk or jog, you will breathe and get in tune with your body. If you walk or jog now, you know what I am talking about. Any kind of cardio workout is good though. Lifting weights or using an elliptical machine or bicycle is also a great way to exercise. You can buy a video and exercise in your house for half an hour or an hour per day. You can buy a yoga video and do yoga in your living room. You can put the radio on and just jump around your living room for twenty minutes every day. Kickboxing videos and classes are very good also. You can do push-ups and sit-ups and squats in your living room. Are you starting to get the point? There is no bad exercise. Exercise is like positive thinking. It is all good for you. Exercise is a positive thing, not a negative thing.

The reason I believe that jogging and walking are the best forms of exercise is because walking and jogging will force you to push your body past its limits, which will in turn teach your brain to be able to push through challenges. When you are walking or jogging and you want to stop but keep going, you are teaching your body to push through. When you walk or jog, you also are putting more and more oxygen into your body and your bloodstream. Most of the mass of the human body is made up of oxygen. The more you exercise, the more oxygen you put into your body. If you jump around your living room listening to music for twenty minutes per day, will you put more oxygen into your body? You better believe it. Walking or jogging will be a steadier flow of breathing and exercise, but any exercise is good.

Exercise is so important because when you exercise, you will also feel better about yourself. What part of your body will make you feel better about yourself? The answer is your brain. When you feel better about yourself, that makes you feel more what? More positive. It all goes hand and hand. Your body and mind are one unit. To become truly positive, you must exercise also. When you exercise, you will be more confident. What is confidence? Confidence is a positive feeling. Do you see where I am going with this? More oxygen, feeling better, teaching your body to push through things, feeling healthy, making the good chemical reactions in your body happen at an optimal level—these are all positive. You must work on making your body a positive body also. Yes, your body can be negative too. You can be unhealthy, which is a negative thing. Being unhealthy physically is negative. You must always be striving toward being healthy, which is positive. It does not matter how you work toward being physically healthy, just like it does not matter how much you are working toward being a positive thinker. It only matters that you are doing something. It is consistency that will lead to being persistent. Persistence will lead to victory. I am purposely keeping this chapter simple because it is important to just know that all exercise is outstanding for you and that working towards having a positive attitude is outstanding for you as well. Then, when you combine the two you will become unstoppable. There are books and literature that are very advanced with exercise and the anatomy of exercise that break down the complex chemical reactions that happen when you exercise. You can dive deep into exercise as you go along on your journey to becoming a truly positive person. The intention here though is for you to understand how important it is to exercise while practicing the other techniques in this book and to know that exercise for the purpose of achieving a positive attitude is one of the techniques that will help you get there.

A lot of people begin to exercise and then stop. I have been going into gyms five to six days per week for over twenty-four years. It is always the same thing, no matter what gym I go into and no matter what city it is in. Every year in January, I see a lot of people that will go to the gym that I have not seen before. Why is this? I call it "a lot of New Year's resolutions." The gym becomes packed every January. This usually lasts until around the end of February, and then what do you think starts happening? I see less and less of the people that I have not seen in the gym in January. Then in late April, the same thing happens. I will see more people again that I do not usually see. What is this? It is because people are trying to get into shape for the summer. Then a couple of months later, I will not see those people anymore either. I have been observing this for the last twenty-four years. Everyone knows that they should be exercising, don't they? We all know that we should be exercising. It is all over the television, commercials, newspapers, magazines. Even our friends are always talking about exercise. It is no secret that we should be exercising. What is the key to weight loss? Eat less and exercise more. No matter where you go and who you talk to about weight loss, if they know about weight loss, they will tell you, "Eat less and exercise more." If that is the case and we all know it, then why do people join the gym in January and stop going after a couple months? They do this because they are not committed. They are not programmed to work out. They are not making working out a priority in their lives. It is also because they are negative thinkers. They let their minds get the best of them. They start saying to themselves things like "I can't do this every day" or "I don't want to exercise today; I can miss one day" or "I would rather be doing something else rather than exercising." People make up reasons why they should not exercise or why it is all right to skip their exercise. Then one day they just stop exercising and tell themselves that they do not have to work out. Their negative, subconscious thoughts overtake their emotional, conscious thoughts. Their subconscious works hard to make them stop working out because they have let their negativity win out in the past.

It sounds crazy that even working out needs to be programmed, but it does. You must push past those negative thoughts that tell you to stop. If you have never worked out, how can you suddenly become an exercise person? It does not happen like that. You are going to have to work out when you do not want to. That is what I must do. That is what everyone I have ever known or talked to about working out has had to do. If I do not want to work out, guess what happens? My subconscious tells me to get in the car and go to the gym. Once I set that in motion, I am fine. Most of the time, I want to work out and look forward to it. But there are those times that I am not very thrilled about it. I know that I should work out and that I must work out because my subconscious tells me that.

Other people can find reasons not to work out when they know they should because their subconscious helps them do that.

So how do you program your mind to want to work out? You do this firstly by telling yourself all the time that you should be working out. Another technique that you will have to practice is visualization. Look in the mirror with your clothes off, and visualize how you would like your body to look. Look at spots that you would like to improve. Look at places on your body that you would like to look different. Visualize yourself in the mirror looking the way you would like to look. Most people out of shape will pass by a mirror with their clothes on and especially with their clothes off and try not to look at it because they do not like the way they look. You need to stop being afraid to look in the mirror. Use the mirror as your friend. Don't be afraid to look in the mirror. Do not be afraid to visualize. You must become your best friend, right? It is important to like what you see when you look in the mirror. Never think negative thoughts when you look in the mirror. When you visualize how you want to look, it will tell your subconscious that you want to look this way. It will make it easier to show up to the gym or to watch a workout video. It will help you get on your bike and go for a bike ride. Visualization will tell your subconscious to make your body look how you are visualizing it. Do this often, and do not be afraid to look in the mirror. Turn the mirror into your friend and know that when you look in the mirror you are looking at your best friend.

When I am at the gym, I am constantly visualizing how I want to look. Sometimes I wonder if people think I am crazy because I am always looking at myself in the mirrors. Most people are afraid to look in the mirrors at the gym because they think others will think they are conceited or vain. I see those people all the time. I am not afraid to look in a mirror no matter where I am. Not because I think I look so good. It is exactly the opposite. It is because I want to visualize how I want to look. If I thought I looked perfect and exactly how I want to, I would not have to look in a mirror, would I? The people that are afraid to look in a mirror are the people that do not like themselves or are afraid of what others will think of them.

As I get older, I am realizing that there is a reason for me to always must visualize what I want to look like. Our bodies are always changing. I am always visualizing and have always had to visualize how I want to look. No matter how much I work out and no matter how much I try, there is always something that I can visualize on my body that I want to work on. This is not because I am compulsive or because I am never satisfied with myself. I am satisfied with myself. It is because our bodies are always changing. This is very exciting! What I am trying to tell you is that you can change your body anytime you want to. Your body is always changing anyways; you might as well change it how you want to. Do you see how exercise goes hand and hand with a positive attitude? When I was a young child, I was so skinny that if the wind blew too hard, I would have been blown away. When I was in my twenties, my body filled out, but it was easy to stay skinny, and I could eat whatever I wanted to. No matter what I ate and how much I ate, I did not gain weight. Then in my thirties, I started to notice that I had to watch what I ate more, and my body started filling out even more. In my late thirties and early forties, I noticed that it was almost difficult to keep weight off. And now, at forty-four, I have to really watch what I eat. I have a secret weapon though. The secret weapon is jogging. Jogging will do so many things for your body, and one of the best things that it does is speed the metabolism up and make you sweat, which will help eliminate toxins and salt.

Sweating is very important for a positive attitude. I can only imagine how much different my life would be if I did not eat healthy and exercise and sweat. If you do not eat right, exercise, and sweat, do not get down on yourself. That is why you are reading this book. You are going to make a change. That is why you are going to read other books now, and you are going to start learning about being a healthy, positive person. You are going to develop discipline in becoming positive and in becoming healthy. Today is the first day of the rest of your life. You do not have to beat yourself up or be hard on yourself—just be consistent. Sweating is very important to living a healthy, positive lifestyle because when you sweat from working out, your body will detoxify itself. By doing this, you will feel better both physically and mentally. Because your brain controls your body, if your body is toxic, your brain as well as your body will not work at an optimal level. The reason I made the name of this book *It's Your Time, It's Your Turn* is because it is time for you to be the best you that you can be. It is your time to feel good physically and mentally at all times. It is your time, and it is your turn.

When you exercise in a manner that makes you sweat and then you are consistent with exercising, something great will happen. You will naturally be able to do a little more each week and push yourself more and more as time goes by. This will make you sweat more and more as time goes by, which will work to detoxify your body and to keep your body detoxified, which will work hand and hand with your other techniques that you practice to achieve a positive attitude. When you exercise and sweat, your body will release endorphins into your body, and your body muscles, joints, and bones will feel better. These are just some of the benefits that will happen if you exercise. Since this not an exercise book, I am not going to go on and on about the benefits of exercise, because the main focus I want you to learn is that one of the benefits to exercise and sweating is a more positive attitude and the ability to develop a truly positive attitude faster. By exercising and sweating as well as eating right and then doing the mental things to become a positive person, your chances of failing are almost zero. When you exercise, sweat, eat right, think positive thoughts, and speak positive words and phrases, you are truly a positive being. It is your time, and it is your turn! This is what I am talking about. As you read this, I know you will understand what I am talking about, and I know that you can imagine what it would be like to achieve what I am describing. Now you must start living this and moving toward this. You now know the things being done by happy, successful, great-looking people whom you have known in the past or may know now. You now know why they are smiling all the time, why they seem to glow. It is not luck. It is not your imagination. They are glowing. There is positive energy coming out of their bodies, which is easily detected by others. It is detected by your subconscious. You just do not always know it is happening, but you know that they have that certain something that you cannot figure out.

When you exercise and sweat consistently, your body will begin to transform. You will see it. It will just happen. Let's talk about this for a moment. I am sure you understand what type of a commitment I am telling you to start. But I want you to think about this. You know that you should be doing these things. Do you know why you know that you should be doing these things? Because your subconscious tells you that you should be. Then when you make excuses of why you do not need to exercise, eat right, and think positively, your subconscious obeys and stops telling you to do the right thing. It concentrates on doing what your conscious mind tells it to. It does this because that is the way your subconscious is programmed. But when your subconscious gets programmed to want to exercise, sweat, and eat right by you making conscious decisions to do these things and then not giving in to negative thoughts of why you should not work out or not eat the right foods, you will see your body transform as well. When you see your body become how you visualize it to look, what do you think will happen to your brain? Your mind will have learned that visualization works, that you can visualize something, and if you put the work into achieving what you visualize, it will happen.

As you work out longer and longer on a consistent level, you will see a transformation happening. It does not matter if you are four hundred pounds or in shape already. It just happens. It is the way the human body operates. If you are overweight or not in the shape you want to be in, it is very important that you understand what I am about to say. When you look in the mirror and do not like what you see, do not be hard on yourself. Be happy with yourself. You have lived your life how you wanted to until this point. Now you are just going to make a change. You can do that, and you have the power to do that. It is your body and your mind. You can do whatever you want with them. Do not be hard on yourself. Do not dwell on the past. Do not beat yourself up over not exercising, not eating the right foods, or not being as healthy as you know you should be. Do not dwell on the past. The past is just that. It is something that has happened, and we can reflect on it as memories and as positive experiences. If we do not like things that have happened in the past, we can then choose to learn from them and change how we do things in the future by analyzing the past and moving forward in a positive way. So, the past should always be positive. Never dwell on the past in a negative manner. If you have not eaten correctly and have not exercised like you wanted to, then make today the day that you are going to change that. Make today the day that you are going to get on a schedule of exercise and eating right. But do not dwell on the past, and do not beat yourself up mentally about not having the willpower and discipline to be at an optimal health level. It is never too late to start, and the past is just that, the past. Love the past, think of the great things that have happened in the past, and learn from the things you want to from the past. Make your past a positive place in your mind. Visualize your body and who you are now as who you should be at this moment, and then visualize your body and your mind as who you want to become. Do not stop visualizing. Never stop visualizing. Wake up every day visualizing and go to bed every night visualizing.

The way you feel about your physical appearance is just as important as how you feel about the way you think and talk. They are all one unit. Your body and mind are connected. I do not know why or how we are on this earth exactly, but I do know that God has a plan for us. I do know that we are the most complex life on earth and that there are millions of species of life on earth. So, if we are the most complex life-forms on a planet as complex as Earth is, then there must be a reason for the way our bodies and minds work. Those of us that understand how our bodies and minds work and use that to our advantage are the people that achieve what they want in life and live the happiest, most fulfilled life. If this is not you, it's your time and it's your turn.

Now let's say that you are overweight and not as healthy as you know you should be. Let's say that you like the way you look when you look in the mirror naked. Maybe when you look in the mirror, you see the perfect person. Then I say to you, do not change a thing. If you look in the mirror every morning and every night before you go to bed and say to yourself, "I am a good-looking human being," then you should not change one thing. If you look in the mirror and do not wish that you were in better shape and truly believe this and are not kidding yourself, then congratulations. You are right where you should be. Everyone is different. I have met people that are happy, and they are not in optimal shape and do not eat perfectly. Life is meant to be lived, so do not think I am saying that you should start eating perfectly tomorrow, go to the gym two hours per day every day, and never speak a negative thing again. You will see in later chapters that I will encourage you to live life to its fullest and try all the things that this earth has to offer. You are here to live. Your reality is what your definition of "living" is. How you perceive living is how you should be programming your subconscious and how you should be living your life. If you are overweight and you know it and if you do not eat right and you know it and you are truly—and I emphasize *truly*—happy with yourself, then you are thinking positive thoughts, aren't you?

I just know that this is not how most of us feel. Most of us want to eat healthy, exercise and want to look good and feel good. Human beings have defined what looks good. There is no secret around the world about what most people think looks good. We know what we like when we look at other people in bathing suits. When someone is in good shape and smiles with their eyes and says positive things all the time and is successful and happy and has the things we want, we all know that we would like that also. There are those people though that truly do not aspire to have monetary things and are happy with what they have. The simple things in life are good enough for them. They are truly happy with the way they look, and they do not want to work out and want to eat the way they want to. I know that there are people like this in the world. I have met them and have analyzed them also. I know that they truly are happy people. If you are one of these people, then you should be very happy because it is not the way most people are. If you are not one of those people though and are like most of the people on earth, then you are going to have to do something about it and learn discipline in the way you think and how you treat your body. The good news is that you are reading this book, and now you are on your way. You should have a huge smile on your face right now, knowing that either way, if you are happy with the way you are right now or if you want to make some changes, you can do it, and you are at the right place, at the right time. It's your time; it's your turn!

Now we are going to move on to talking about the way you should be eating. I suggest that you buy some books and do some research on exercising and maybe even sign up to be with a personal trainer at your local gym if you have never exercised before. Do not stop learning about exercise. I am always learning about exercise and how my body is changing. I am always concentrating on how to make my body work on an optimal level. I know that as I get older, my body will change and my hormones will change, which will make the way I exercise and eat change as well. You need to learn what that means for your body. You can only do this by analyzing it and talking to your doctor and other people that know more about this than you. You can only do this by doing it every day. You must try different types of workouts and exercises to find out what will work best for your body. But one thing that is a consistent by-product of working out is sweating. And one thing that is a constant by-product of sweating is a more positive body and mind. You should always be striving to have a positive body and mind. Just always be moving toward a more positive body and mind. Visualize yourself as looking and thinking that way you would like to. Then go get what you want! Know that there are going to be setbacks and that life is going to throw challenges and obstacles in your way. Know that you are not going to always be perfect. Know that you are not perfect, and that the world is not a perfect place. Do not beat yourself up or dwell on the past. Just decide to always be striving toward having a positive body and mind. Make it simple. It is simple.

Eating right and exercising go hand in hand, so I want to cover them in one chapter. They are one and the same. If you are eating right but not exercising or working out but not eating right, you are not truly being positive physically. If you are doing one of these things but not the other, you are halfway there, which is better than not doing either of them. Just like if you are eating right and exercising but not thinking positively, you are not truly being a positive person. "You are what you eat." Yes, this saying is true. We are what we eat. Let's look at how we are eating. I love food. I love all types of food. There are really no foods that I do not like. I like foods that are bad for me more than foods that are good for me. I love pizzas, pastas, hamburgers, French fries, sodas, cheeses, breads, fried chicken, fried foods, chicken wings, salty foods, sweet foods, and on and on. But if I like all foods, that means I like foods that are good for me too, right? I am sure you are the same way. You probably like most foods, and you like healthy foods also, foods like vegetables, chicken, lean meats, fish, and fruits. Maybe you do not eat meat and eat plant-based meat substitutes. These are all good foods too. For some reason though, we are constantly bombarded by foods that are not good for us. It is on TV, in the supermarkets, on the Internet, on billboards while we are driving. It is everywhere. Why is that? It is simple. Companies understand that by constantly having their products in front of you, it will work on your subconscious to make you want to try their product. And then when you try those products, they put special ingredients in them that they know your brain will want more of, so you will want to buy their products more. Now that you know this, all you have to do is observe what I am saying, and you will see what I am talking about.

As I have said before, life is meant to be lived. I am a firm believer that we should be enjoying all of what life has to offer to us. Life is meant to be lived. I have met people that do not eat meat, fast food, fried foods, pizza, bread, or anything else that is considered unhealthy. I wonder to myself, "What are these people missing out on?" I could not imagine living life without fried foods, cheeses, nachos, breads, sodas, and everything else that we all love that is not good for us. Life is meant to be lived. The answer to my question though is that they are not missing out on anything because they are feeling positive about the way they are eating and living. They are not missing out on anything. But with moderation, all foods can be eaten. Look at foods That are not very healthy as treats, not the kind of food that you eat day in and day out. Does that make sense? It is perspective. More and more people today are deciding to eat only certain foods and eat a certain way such as eating no meat and no dairy, or no meat fish but dairy, etc. There is no right or wrong for the sake of this book and what you are achieving by its techniques. There is only a healthy diet and a non-healthy diet. You must determine what that exactly means for you, but we all know what foods are bad for us and good for us in the basic sense. Start doing some research on foods. Try different diets and different foods and see how you feel. Talk with your doctor, with trainers and other people to get ideas. My perspective of food is that I need to be eating healthy foods most of the time and eat foods that are not healthy only sometimes if I want to look the way I would like to look and if I want to be a truly positive person. I must practice discipline, and having done this my entire life, I have programmed my subconscious to make me feel guilty if I eat bad foods too much. I will not enjoy them if I eat them too much. My subconscious knows what I want, and even if I try to make conscious decisions to eat bad foods too much, I cannot. You must become the same way. You do this by taking it one day at a time, one meal at a time. This is what people do not know. Just like with positive thinking. There is a secret to looking good and eating healthy; otherwise, everyone would look perfect, right? There would not be so many weight loss products and gimmicks on TV. There would not be so many workout videos or infomercials every night while you are lying in bed. What people that eat right know that you may not is that you must concentrate on eating right one meal at a time. Then you go from there. It all starts by being disciplined one meal at a time. The same thing goes for having a positive attitude. If you recall the last chapters, thinking positive begins by one conversation with yourself or others at a time. You also must know that life is meant to be lived and that you cannot beat yourself up for slipping and not being perfect. You must shrug setbacks off and move forward. This is what successful, happy people do.

I bet if you observe the people that you know or are around all day that glow and are truly happy and successful, they eat right most of the time. They practice discipline with food. I also bet if you talked to them about food, they would tell you that they love to eat bad foods too. I bet they could reel off many foods that are bad for us that they love to eat: ice cream, candy, soda, pizza, fried food, and on and on. We all love foods that are bad for us. The trick is to be disciplined and visualize how we want to look and then eat the foods that are going to make us look how we want to look while exercising and thinking positive thoughts. When you eat right, you will feel much better about yourself, and you will be achieving your goals and your visualizations of how you want to look, which will reinforce your positive attitude. Doing all these three things will make you a truly positive person. Think about this for a moment. Put the book down now, and think about what I just said. There are three things in your life that you must change to become a truly positive person and to have the things you want and to be who you want. Three things. Not ten things, not twenty things—three things. That is, it. Once you change these three things, then everything else will fall into place. These three things are the foundation for those people that you know that are successful. This is the secret that they know that you did not know until now. There is one more thing that I am going to add in a later chapter, which is dreaming, but dreaming stems from being positive and healthy. Exercise, eating right, and thinking and speaking positive thoughts all the time are the three basics to everything good in life.

So, what kinds of foods should you be eating? Let me start by saying that everyone's body is different. It is important that you get to know your body, consult your doctor, read books on nutrition and body types, and do research on dieting and exercise, but I am here to give you the basics and the knowledge that diet and exercise are essential to being positive. I am going to tell you what foods I have found to be the best for me and what other people have told me they are eating in order to lose weight and feel better. I have worked with people that are nutritionists, and I have read books on food, exercise, and diet. I have also been exercising and eating right since I can remember what kinds of food I ate. My mother used to cook for me every night. I did not eat out at all. My mother would cook good foods, healthy foods. So, I acquired a taste for healthy foods, foods like lean meats, vegetables, good carbohydrates, and salads. When my mother took me to a fast-food restaurant, it was a treat, not how I ate every day. I ate breakfast, lunch, and dinner at home most of the time. Are you doing this? Are you doing this for your children? It is the foundation of eating right.

As I am getting older, I am realizing that the foods I once was able to eat every day I cannot now, foods like pastas, rice, and breads. My body is changing, and my metabolism is slowing down. What is working for me now is not how I had to eat in my early twenties and my early thirties. What I have found to be the most effective way to keep my weight down and feel the best is to not eat a lot of carbohydrates, carbohydrates like pasta, white rice, and bread. I have learned that vegetables are carbohydrates also, and because I do not have an active career, I do not need to eat carbohydrates like breads, rice, and pastas with every meal. When I stick to this plan, I notice that my weight goes down and stays down. This is what works for me now. You must find out what works for you, but I am sharing this with you because most of the people that I know that are losing weight are cutting down on carbohydrates. Most of the commercials on television about diets are low-carbohydrate diets. It seems to work. What I also have learned is that our bodies need carbohydrates, so do not go without any carbohydrates. That is not good for you either. We need carbohydrates for energy and brainpower. Now put the book down again and write on your paper that you look at every day: "I am going to exercise daily. I am going to sweat when I exercise. I am going to eat right, and I am going to practice discipline with food, and I am going to feel awesome!"

When you exercise regularly and eat a diet that works for you to keep your weight down, you will then force your body to become a positive body. Your muscles, joints, skin, and organs will work at an optimal level, which will help your positive attitude. I cannot explain how much of a good feeling this becomes once you do this, but I can tell you that when you do this and achieve a true positive state, you will know it. You will feel as though you are floating, not walking. You will have a smile on your face all the time. You will feel happy. It is one of those things that you will just feel, and when you do, you will remember reading this and say, "That is what he was talking about." It is better than any drug or alcohol. It is a feeling of goodness that does not go away. There is no crash. There is no hangover. As a matter of fact, the feeling just gets better and better as you get more positive and healthier. It is true happiness. It is a true sense of self-achievement. Then what will happen is you will treat others around you better because you will feel good about yourself. You will become the person that others observe and wonder what you have that they do not.

There is one more component to feeling physically healthy. You need to take a good multivitamin. As with everything, ask your doctor about this first, but I believe that everyone should take a good multivitamin. Not just any multivitamin, but a good one. There are big differences in vitamins. Learn about vitamins, and try different vitamins. Pay attention to how they make you feel and then what is on the label. Go to stores and ask about the vitamins. The people that work in vitamin stores will guide you and teach you about vitamins. But if you are not taking a multivitamin, then ask your doctor if you should be taking one, and if they say yes, go get some immediately. Once you become a truly positive person, you will take more risks, be more active, and your mind will race with ideas and thoughts. Your body, mind, and soul will light up like a lightbulb. You become alive. You will be working out, pushing your body and pushing your mind because challenges get you up. It is very difficult to eat all the foods every day, day in and day out, that your body needs to run on an optimal level. As a matter of fact, it is almost impossible. I have been taking the best vitamins I can get my hands on since I graduated from high school and could buy my own vitamins. I learned at a very early age how much different a good multivitamin can make me feel. When I do not take my vitamins, I notice within one or two weeks that I do not feel the same. I have less energy and less motivation. What happens is when you take a multivitamin, your body will use the vitamins and supplements that it needs, and you lose the ones that you do not need when you urinate. It is really that simple. If you do not take vitamins now and you buy some, give yourself about two weeks to feel the difference. If you have not felt the difference in two weeks or after you finish the bottle, you are probably not taking a multivitamin that works for you. Try a different type. Do not buy a two-or three-month supply of vitamins at first until you find one you like.

Taking a multivitamin will help keep your immune system working in peak performance, and it will also help your brain to think better, be sharper, and yes, be more positive. When you are getting all the vitamins and minerals that your body requires, you will feel more positive and physically better. You only live once, and you need every advantage you can get to be what you want to be and have what you want to have in life. This is your life, and you deserve to feel incredible every day, and you deserve to be happy. You deserve to feel like you are living a fulfilled life and the life that you choose to live while being truly happy. Do not be cheap with a multivitamin. Good multivitamins that you will feel are not cheap. Always buy a whole food multi. Do this for yourself. Do not go without vitamin and mineral supplements. If you are a person that cannot take multivitamins, your doctor tells you that you should not be taking them for some reason, or you just do not want to take a multivitamin, then do not stress out. Just eat better. Eat more fruits, vegetables, nuts and good proteins. Take that kind of food to work with you, and eat them throughout the day. Just eat better. You must make a conscious effort to eat better and eat the right foods if you cannot take multivitamins. You are going to have to learn about eating the right foods, and do the same thing as if you were taking a multivitamin. Eat different types of fruits and vegetables at different times of the day to see what make you feel the best. But either way, you need to be doing one of these things. We do not eat right in America, as in most other countries. Eating right is a big part of becoming a truly positive person.

Hopefully, you are seeing how important exercise and diet are to a positive attitude. They go hand in hand. If you are always striving to look the way you would like to look and feel the way you would like to feel physically, then you will be telling your subconscious when you talk to yourself that you have discipline, high self-esteem, and are living your life how you choose to. You will be telling yourself every day that you like the way you look and that you are proud of yourself for having the discipline to exercise and eat right and to be healthy physically. Make sure if you slip up or have times that you are not able to exercise or you eat foods that you know you should not be eating; you do not beat yourself up for it. Just smile, look in the mirror, laugh, and say to yourself, "I am human, and I am not perfect." Give yourself a pat on the back, and be proud of yourself for trying to live a healthy life, and then tell yourself that you are going to get back on your routine. It is that simple. You no longer beat yourself up or get caught up in negative thoughts and actions. You are human, and you will make mistakes, and you are not perfect. No one is. Also, love who you are now, even while you are becoming who you want to be.

Another part of your diet that you should always control is alcohol and drugs. Alcohol and drugs are among the most negative things that you can do to your brain and your body. If you learn about the effects that drugs and alcohol have on your brain and your body, you will see that the side effects are depression of some kind. Drugs and alcohol make your brain release endorphins, serotonin, just to mention a few chemicals, which make you feel good for some time. But then after the drug wears off, there are consequences to pay for that. Part of those consequences is negativity and depression of some kind. There are also physical consequences to pay as well. Now I am going to throw a curveball at you. Now that you know this, it is important that you live your life. It is important that you do things that you like to do. Life is meant to be lived. If you enjoy having drinks occasionally, getting together with friends, listening to music, eating good foods, and being social, then you should do that. I strongly suggest that you do things that make you happy.

I have had many good times in my life while having drinks with friends. One thing I have practiced is moderation. Moderation is very important. If you drink alcohol every day, you will feel the effects of it, and you will not achieve a truly positive state. I suggest you never do drugs, but if you do, you will feel the effects in a negative way, and you will not be able to achieve a truly positive state. It is important to limit drinking and have discipline with drinking, the same way you must practice discipline with food, negative thoughts, and exercise.

Alcohol is just something we consume. It is part of our diet or not part of our diet. Think of it that way. If you eat cheeseburgers, French fries, pizzas, chicken fingers, pastas, and sodas every meal, what will happen to you? What will you look like? How will you feel? The same is true for alcohol. If you do not drink alcohol, then you are way ahead of the game, but if you do like to have drinks with your friends, then control it. Never stop yourself from having good times and doing things that make you happy. Having good times and doing things you enjoy are positive and will build positive memories for your subconscious to have. That is good for you. Just know that alcohol and drugs are depressants, and anything in your life that is a depressant is negative. You must find the balance and listen to your body and mind. Once you begin to think positive thoughts all the time, you will understand more what I am talking about, but for now, just make sure to practice moderation.

While you are making this transformation, it is important for you to enjoy the journey. It is important for you to love who you are now. You must love yourself now. Love the way you look. No matter how you look now. You are just going to begin moving toward the person that you would like to become. Do not hate the person you were or are now. Enjoy today, enjoy yesterday, and enjoy the journey ahead of you. Be humble, and do not think you are better than anyone because you now know the secrets that successful, truly happy people know. Once you experience what I am talking about and truly believe it works, tell others and do not keep it to yourself. Helping others will make you become who you want to become faster. Today is just that, today. Yesterday was just that, yesterday. But tomorrow is a different day. You can make tomorrow whatever you want of it. Accept yourself for who you were, who you are, and know that you can make tomorrow any way you want to. Ask God to help you get there and to show you the way. When you do all this, how can you fail? You cannot. You may slip up, stop for one reason or another, but you will not lose tomorrow. You will always have another tomorrow until the day you die.

CHAPTER 6

Money

"Every morning in Africa, a gazelle wakes up. It knows it must run faster than the fastest lion or it will be killed. Every morning a lion wakes up. It knows it must outrun the slowest gazelle or it will starve to death. It doesn't matter whether you are a lion or a gazelle. When the sun comes up, you'd better be running."

Put this saying on your paper you read every day. Live by this rule. When the sun comes up, are you running? Do you live like there may not be a tomorrow? Do you have a sense of urgency? Or do you wake up and wish you could just go back to bed and sleep more? Money is something that can be looked at as something positive or negative, can't it? You can look at money in many ways. But no matter how you look at money, you cannot deny that money is needed for survival. I look at money as security. The more I have of it, the more secure I feel. This is not the right or wrong way to look at money; it is just my perspective of money. I find it interesting that I look at money as security. It is just something that happened in my programming when I was younger, and I have never changed it. I like my perspective of money. It keeps me motivated to make more. It also makes me not think of money as a bad thing. It does not make me feel like I am better than people who have less money than I have and beneath people that have more money than I do. It also is a positive way to look at money. Security is a positive emotion.

I described my perspective of money to give you an example of how people look at money. Money is something that is always going to have to be in your life until someone changes the way the world gathers things. But in our lifetimes, we are most likely going to be stuck with money. I do not love the way the world is set up with currency, jobs, and who has the most money has the most things. I have spent some time wondering what the world would be like without money and what a better system of how humans live and survive would be, but I cannot really think of one. Money and doing things to gather money seem to be a pretty good way for humans to keep themselves in check and for the most amount of harmony between humans on earth. I do believe that someday there will not be a system of currency for trade around the world. It will be many years from now, maybe even hundreds or thousands of years. I think that humans will evolve past money and trading money for items. But for now, this is what we all must deal with. Why not make it a positive experience? It is very important to make all things that you must do day in and day out and things you must think about day in and day out positive. Money is one of those things.

The reason money is in a positive-thinking book is because money can be such a negative thing. Money can really make your world seem dark and unhappy, can't it? We all have experienced times of wondering where we were going to get our next dollar. It is important that you look at money in a positive way. I have talked to people that hate money and all that it stands for. It is OK not to care about money. Just do not look at money as a negative thing. You will always have to deal with money as long as you are alive. Money is a constant in our lives. If you do not care about having money and do not desire having things that money can buy, do not think you are crazy. All that is important in your life from this day forward is that you live your life how you want to live it and do not have regrets. Never worry about what other people think about you. Your opinion of yourself is the only opinion that matters. If you like yourself, others will like you too. If you do not care about money, do not care about it. You do not have to change that, but just make sure that you do not look at money as a negative thing. Accept that money is part of being alive and that you need it to survive. Money is not a bad thing. It is just money. Do not despise money because some people have more than you or because you wish you had more of it. Just tell yourself often that you are going to have all the money you want. Put the book down and write this on your paper that you read every day: "I look at money as a positive thing, and I do not worry about what other people have. I only worry about what I have and what I want that money can buy. I will have all the things in life that I want and all the money I want in time. I will do what it takes to achieve this, and I will think positive thoughts and enjoy the journey while achieving my goals that involve money and what money can buy."

If success to you is having money and the things that money can buy, then I will give you some secrets to money that you do not know about. The number one and most important thing that people do not know about money is that when you are truly a positive person and achieve a positive attitude, you will make more money. When you are truly positive, you will attract money. Money comes to people that believe they deserve to make money and have money. As you become more positive, you will believe that you deserve to have the things in life you want. The law of attraction will then take place within you, and you will begin to attract the things that you want and desire. The explanation for this is energy. There is energy everywhere around us. Money is attracted to positive energy. And positive energy is attracted to money. This does not mean that you need to have money because you become truly positive. Maybe you do not care about money and your desire in life is to live in another country in a village with no running water and electricity and fight diseases for the poor. Maybe you would like to live under a bridge and not talk to anyone or have anything. That is OK. That does not make you any less of a person than someone that wants to have their own jet, yacht, and houses on beaches. That is the beauty of being human. That is the beauty of money. We can live our lives how we choose to live them. When you are positive, though, and think positive thoughts, you will then be able to attract the money you are going to need to move to another country and help fight disease in a poor village with no running water, as well as have lots of money or a foundation that will raise money to help many people that are in need. If you aspire to live under a bridge and have nothing, you will still need to eat every day, have items to shower with, and other items to survive. Either way you look at money, whether you are a lion or a gazelle, you must hit the ground running every morning when the sun comes up. If you work on a night shift, you will have to hit the ground running every night when the sun goes down. Lions and gazelles are up at night also.

It is important that you learn to save money. Have you ever observed people that never have money? They are always unhappy and stressed out. They try to be positive, but they are always stressed out. When you have a little money saved up, you will look at money in a more positive manner and be less stressed out about money. You may say, "But I cannot save money because I do not make enough money to save any." I am not talking about saving any certain amount of money. I am talking about saving something. Can you save one penny per day? Can you save five cents or twenty-five cents per day? Can you save ten dollars per paycheck? Think about it. You can save something if you really want to. If you do not have one, go and open a savings account tomorrow. Put the minimum amount in it that you are required to open one. Then just save something in there every paycheck. Set a goal for yourself, and put a little bit in there every paycheck. The reason you need to have a separate account from your checking account is because you should spend the money in your checking account and not spend the money in your savings account. Do you understand? We must have a separation in accounts in order to save money. If you know that you have a savings account that you do not spend money out of, you will be more apt not to spend it. You will program your subconscious to not want to spend money out of the savings account as time goes by. You will also be more apt to save more money in it.

Saving money is like learning a skill. The more money you save, the more money you will want to save. The same goes for spending money. When you start spending money all the time, it can get out of control, can't it? When you save money, you will notice that you feel good about yourself. You will feel good about your life. You will feel a sense of achievement and learn discipline. This will help you with teaching yourself how to be positive all the time. Everything I am going to talk about in this book goes hand in hand. It is all related. As you fine-tune your skill of saving money, many good things will happen for you. You will feel more positive about your life. You will also be able to have things that you would not have if you did not save money. You will also be able to do things that you would not do if you did not save money. Money has a funny way of being spent on things you really do not need and really do not want, doesn't it? It makes us feel good to spend money. Money is meant to be spent. But when you save money, you will find that you are able to have different and better things than when you did not save money.

When you are saving money, it is important to treat yourself and reward yourself by buying yourself something every so often with the money you save. You will then be practicing the discipline of delayed gratification. Delayed gratification will also help you to dream and will teach you that good things come to those who wait. As you get better at delayed gratification, you will also realize that the longer you wait to treat yourself with something while saving money, the better and larger of an item you will be able to get for you or the more fun you will able to have, like going on a vacation. All these are positive actions. When you do not save money and always spend extra money on things that you do not really need or do things you do not really need to do, that is negative. Doing this can cause guilt. It can cause you to have negative conversations with yourself. It is much like not being able to eat right or not exercising when you know you should. It is like not being able to think positive thoughts all the time when you know you should be. All this is related. It can also affect your relationships in a negative manner. It is time to become a positive person with money. We all know that we should be saving money. The difference between people that understand money and how money works and the people that do not is that they learn to save money and then learn how to make money work for them. There are many millionaires that started with almost no money. There are many millionaires that have lost everything and had no money at all, only to rebuild their dynasty again. It does not matter what job you have or what your circumstances are. You do not have to have money to make money. You must have a positive attitude, know how to practice delayed gratification, and believe that positive energy will attract money to have more money. And above all, you must be your own best friend and feel that you deserve to have everything that you desire in your lifetime, no matter what it is. You deserve it!

When you save money, something else will happen for you as well. When you have some money in a savings account, you are more apt to take risks. Risks will not seem as scary to you when you know you have some money to fall back on. When you take risks, you will get rewarded. The more risks you take, the more rewards you will receive. I will talk later about risks and how to overcome the fear of risks, but for now, just know that when you save money, you will be more apt to take risks. Once you truly achieve a positive attitude, you will then be able to take risks and overcome fears, which will make you money and give you success while achieving your goals. When you combine that with being able to save money and practice delayed gratification, you will be on your way to success, no matter what success means to you. You will be able to turn this positive money-making machine in your brain on and off at will. This will take a lot of practice, the same as becoming a truly positive, happy person. The good news is that this can be done simultaneously and as part of your positive-attitude training because it all goes hand in hand. It is all positive.

The reason it is important to talk about money in this book is because if you let money become a negative factor in your life, it can consume you. Money is a constant in our lives. We must keep our perspective of money a positive one. That does not mean we have to love money or worship money, but we only have to have a positive perspective of money. When I think of money, I think of other things besides security. I look at money as a way to have things I want, like, and enjoy doing. I always look at money as a positive part of my life. What I like about money is that I can make as much as I choose to in my lifetime. I can make just enough money to get me by every month if I choose, or I can aspire to be the richest man on earth. Money is what I want from it. I do not get caught up in thinking about what other people have that I do not. I know there will always be someone that has more than me and less than me. I only worry about my own finances. I never worry about keeping up with my friends and other people. I stay in my own world and my own mind with money. I do not let anyone influence me. I will talk more about how I do this and how you need to do this in later chapters.

I will never forget the day I saw the looks on the faces of the people that worked at my company one day when I bought a new car for myself. Most of the people that worked at the company made pretty good money. The year was 2002. I was making a substantial amount of money every month, and the people that I worked with knew it. I spent about three months looking at all kinds of cars. Then one day, I drove up to my office with a burgundy Honda Accord. It was brand-new, and I paid cash for it, and the car was all mine. I negotiated a great price, and I had paid for a car. I was proud of my Accord. The first day I drove it to my office, I told the people that worked there that I bought a new car and that it was in the parking lot. They all immediately wanted to see and said, "Let's go look at your new car!" I led everyone to the parking lot, and we walked to my covered parking spot, and there sat my new burgundy Honda Accord. All of them began to laugh at me. They looked at me like I was crazy. They were laughing because they knew I could have any car I wanted, but I drove up in a Honda Accord and was proud of it. All the people that worked at my company had nicer cars than I did. They began to call me a cheapskate and a crazy man for driving a Honda Accord. "The owner of one of the most successful mortgage companies in the city does not drive a Honda Accord," they said. I was supposed to be driving a high-end BMW, Mercedes, Jaguar, Audi, or a Porsche. What they did not know, and I did not tell them, was that I was practicing delayed gratification. By having paid for a

Honda Accord, I saved gas, insurance rates, maintenance, and did not have to worry about needing a new car for many years, and it gave me the ability to save much more money as the years went on. What they did not know is that I wanted to buy my own office building and put my company in the building. I wanted to take some risks in business that they did not know about. Practicing delayed gratification and saving money allowed me to do these things. As they laughed, I laughed too because I knew that I looked crazy driving that car, but I did not think one negative thought because I was programmed to look at practicing delayed gratification in a positive manner and to never worry about what others think about me. I bought a building two years later, moved my company into it.

Try to never let money get in the way of your dreams and your relationships. I know that is much easier said than done, but you must tell yourself that. Write that down on your piece of paper that you read every day. "I will not let money get in the way of my dreams and my relationships." I will talk more about money and relationships and money and dreams, but for now just write that down on your piece of paper and read it every day. Do not let money get in the way of having a good time in life. Never think that because you do not have the amount of money you would like or if you do not make the amount of money you want to, you cannot enjoy your life. Always tell yourself that you have a great life and that you may want more but that at this time you are happy with your life. Life is short, and it is going to go by very fast. I have had both young and old people tell me all the time how fast life is passing them by. Think about this for a minute. Every year you celebrate New Year's Eve, then before you know it, it is March. Then the summer goes by and Halloween comes. Then Thanksgiving and Christmas come, and you are celebrating New Year's Eve again. Doesn't it seem like your year goes by like that? I know it does for me and everyone else I talk to. Now think of this. If you are lucky enough to live to ninety, you only get to do this about seventy-five times in your lifetime because you do not pay attention to how the years go by until you are around fifteen years old. That is why life goes by so fast. Ninety years is not that long of a time to be on this earth. Our planet is approximately

4.5 billion years old. Our lives are less than a grain of sand in the ocean timewise on earth. Make sure that you spend your precious time on earth happy and without regrets. Every day when the sun comes up, make sure you are running and make sure you are living like there may not be a tomorrow. When you do this, and you do it with a positive attitude you will have as much money as you desire in life. Doors will open for you that you could only dream of. You will see and make opportunities for yourself that you think can only happen to rich, successful people. You are going to be no different than those that have everything they desire in life and look happy all the time, smile with their eyes, stand up straight and exude an aura of self-confidence and success.

Now that you have read this about money, I am sure it makes perfect sense to you. I am sure that by now you are saying to yourself, "I think if I did all these things I have learned in this book, my life would be better." Let me tell you that you would be right. There is only one catch to it all. Only one catch. Usually something spectacular in life has many catches, but these secrets I am sharing with you only have one catch. The catch is that you are going to have to believe it will happen, experience it happening to you, and the only way this will happen to you is if you try it and practice it for as long as it takes to change your programming. That is the only catch to this new, wonderful, exciting, positive life. The only catch is that you must make a decision to do it. Once it goes from your head to your heart and then back to your head again, a seed will be planted, and as you water that seed, the plant will grow into a huge, healthy tree with deep roots everywhere. You are going to have be patient with yourself, make mistakes, and even practice at saving money and being positive with money.

From this day forward, you should be having positive conversations with yourself about money. When you think about money to yourself, think of money as a positive part of your life. Look at money as something that you must have but do not need to make you happy. Find something that money does for you or can do for you that is positive and makes you feel good, and then dwell on that always when you think about money. Find other ways that money is good in your life and think of only those things when you think of money. If you catch yourself thinking about money in a negative manner, stop that right away. Change the conversation you are having with yourself in your head, and look at the positive things that money does for you, your family, and your life. If you are having a hard time to stop thinking negatively, stop the conversation in your head immediately. Start over or think about something else. Teach yourself that if you cannot think positive thoughts about something for some reason, you will simply think about something else, or you will stop the conversation in your head and reset it to a positive conversation. This is exactly what you must do when you are having a conversation with another person or if you are speaking in front of thousands of people. If you are talking about money with other people, do not engage in and never start a negative conversation with people. Only have positive conversations with people about money. If you find that you are in a conversation about money with others and it is a negative conversation, when it is your turn to talk, do not fuel the fire by talking negative also. Say something positive about money, and watch others in the conversation begin to do the same. You will have to practice this for as long as it takes, but you can be sure that if you do, as time goes by, you will master this technique and it will help change your life forever. Remember, practice makes perfect, and do not be hard on yourself if you are having a hard time staying away from negative thoughts and conversations about money. You have programmed yourself to think and talk this way about money your entire life. You will not reprogram yourself overnight.

Money is something in your life that you will not be able to escape. If you live by yourself, sit down soon and take a piece of paper and a pen out and write down everything that you must pay each month. Not just your bills, but everything you need, want, and do each month. Take some time to gather this information so you do not miss anything. If you do miss something, add to your list. You should put down all your expenses, like car payments, house payments, electricity, gas, phone, car insurance, etc. Write down all your bills that you have each month. Then figure out and write down any bills you pay yearly or quarterly. Write down all your bills that you pay throughout the course of a year. Then write down how much money you spend each month on food. If you do not know, take some time and figure it out, even if you must take a month or two and keep track of your grocery bill every month. Then do the same thing with how much money you spend on entertainment and doing things on your day off and vacations and anything else you do each month that is not a bill or groceries. Write down how much you spend on items monthly or yearly for your house, condo, or apartment. Then write down how much you spend on clothes each month or each year. Then write down how much you spend on personal items that are not food, like deodorant, shampoo, hair spray, makeup, soap, laundry and dish detergent, etc. If you include these items when you shop for groceries, then keep it part of your grocery bill. Then write down anything else you spend your money on each month or yearly. Think of everything you spend money on each month and try not to miss anything.

Once you have everything you spend money on each month and each year written down, total up how much you spend per month, and then multiply that by twelve to get a yearly amount. If you have only a yearly amount, divide it by twelve to get a monthly amount. If you are single, do this for yourself, and if you are in a relationship or married, do this as a couple. Figure out how much you spend monthly and yearly as a couple. Then once you have that on paper, write down how much money you or both of you make per month and per year. Then look at that piece of paper. Do not say anything. Do not argue with yourself or with anyone else about what is on the paper. Remember as you are doing this that this is a positive exercise. Make it positive, and keep it positive until the end. Do not engage in any negative thoughts or conversations about this exercise. As you look at the paper, analyze it for a few days or a few weeks. Reflect on your life, your thoughts about money, and about the items and things you spend your money on every month and every year. Look at your life. Your life will be on that piece of paper. How you make money, how much money you make each month, and what you buy, have, and do to spend it on each month will be on there also. Most likely, it will look different than what you think about as your life each day. You will finally see what your life really looks like. Putting things down on paper is very important. It is what successful, happy, positive people know about. It is one of the little things that make a huge difference in being positive and successful.

After you have a list of your income and expenses and you take a while to look at everything and analyze your life, it will then be time to go to work on your list and to say to yourself either "I like how I am living my life" or "I need to make some changes that I see on this list and in my life." Just like everything else I describe in this book, do not be hard on yourself. Do not argue with your spouse about this list. This is a positive exercise. If you do not like what you see on that list, pat yourself on the back and put a huge smile on your face. Be proud of yourself and be happy because now you have a working list of your life. You now know what your life looks like financially. You do not have to guess any longer. You do not have to look at money as anything but what it is. Money is something on your list that you can control, and you can make what you want of. Your list of what you spend money on every month and every year is now something that is tangible, and you can do what you want with it now. You can add things to it, take things off it. You can change your budget and change your life in any way you want to. You will have to practice at this, and you will have to learn to work on a list and look at your life in this way, but once you do and once you master this technique, you will be in control of your life, and you will no longer look at money as a negative thing in your life. You will be in control of money; money will no longer control you. You will be in control of your thoughts and conversations about money. You will know where you stand with money. You will know that money is something that works for you and is something that you can see clearly in your head. Your perspective of money will then be clear. You will be able to plan for things that you want and what it will take with the amount of money you make. You will also be able see how much more money you will need to make in the future to have additional things you want in your life, no matter how large or small. And you will be able to see what you can eliminate from your list to have more money each month and year. Always keep this list working. Make sure that you are always adding and subtracting to your list. Look at your list often, and tell yourself that your list is going to be with you for years and for the rest of your life. Money is now a positive thing in your life.

By making a list of your income and liabilities and expenses, you will be able to face money for what it is. You will no longer be afraid of money. Money will not scare you and make you feel nervous. When we face our fears and ask ourselves, "What is the worst thing that can happen from this scenario?" we then work on making that scenario better because we have faced the worst it can throw at us. You may feel uncomfortable at first or nervous or scared or angry when you complete your list. Look at that in a positive way. You got it out. You do not have to spend your days, every payday, every month end, every birthday, every Christmas thinking about money and where it is going to come from. You will now know where you are at financially. That may be an uncomfortable feeling when you first complete your list, but the positive side to that is you have now faced the worst-case scenario with your finances. That list is the worst that it can get. Now all you must do is change the list into how you want it and make it a positive list. It may take a while. It may take a year or two, but you have something to work on now, and money will become your friend. Money will help you change your list to a positive list. Money will help you make your life better. You can also make more money somehow if you choose to add bills or things you spend money on each month to your list. You will see that you control money. You can make as much or as little as you want. The only thing you must know is how that will affect your list, which is your life.

When I was nineteen, I owned my own house, had a full set of bills, a car payment, and all the expenses that went along with it. For some reason, I always had a working list of how much money I made, how much money I spent, and how much money I could save. All I really did is take all the figures from my head and write it down. That is all you must do. Now I own three businesses and have many bills and different types of incomes to write down and keep track of. I now have money programs and bookkeepers and a payroll company to help me keep track of the money I bring in or even lose each month, and the money I spend each month. But my household finances are still done the same way as I have described. I have been doing this so long that I can almost do it in my sleep. I can see the list in my head because I have been doing this for more than fifteen years. Just about a year ago, I sat down and made a list of all the expenses in my household each month and how much money had to be put in the bank account for the household bills each month. I wanted to see how close I was in my head, and I wanted to make sure I was not missing anything. After fifteen years of doing this, I still use a piece of paper and a pen to manage my money and my perspective of money.

Now that you know all this about money, make sure you do all these things, and start right now. Put the book down and close your eyes. Think about all the things you have learned in this chapter, and tell yourself that you are going to start implementing these things into your life right away. Tell yourself that you are going to learn more about money. Read books and talk to people that know more than you about money. You are going to go to seminars on money to learn more about it. Now that you know money is something that can be a very negative or positive force in your life, it is time to make sure that it is always positive. If you are doing some of these things already or all these things, then put the book down and smile and be thankful that you are already doing things to look at money from a positive perspective. Tell yourself that you are going to never stop learning about money and thinking about money in a positive way. If you do not care about money and do not want it to be something that you think about always in your life, then tell yourself that you meant that and that you will not stress out about money, and you will live your life the way you want to and never worry about what others think about money. When you put the book down and close your eyes, also take a moment to think about everything else you have learned in this book and how they are all related. Look at it all in your head, and start visualizing how everything in your life can be looked at through a negative mind and negative eyes or a positive mind and positive eyes. Think about it for a while. Analyze it. You have taken in a lot of information, and money is a huge part of our lives. Your changing your perspective on money will be a big deal. You will also have to help others in your life change their perspective as well. This is not a short and easy task. It will take discipline, practice, and the belief that it can and will happen! Think about all this when you put the book down. Tell yourself that you are going to have to be consistent and patient and that this is a marathon, not a sprint. Money is going to be in your life until the day you die. You have the rest of your life to get this right, but you want to live life like there is no tomorrow. Now put the book down, close your eyes, and enjoy!

CHAPTER 7

Relationships

If you think about what human beings do throughout their lifetimes, there are some things that we all have in common, and there are some things that we all do and what our lives revolve around. For most people, these things are the same. They are the things that we do every day, and they are the things that we must do to survive every day. If you think about it, what do our lives really consist of? We all eat food, drink fluids, sleep. We must have shelter. We must have money, and we have relationships, sex, and children. Then there are the other things that we do every day and that money can provide. Most of us have a job or a career to gather money and items that we want in our lives. So, our lives really revolve around food, sleep, relationships, sex, children, money, items we want to have, and shelter. If you think about it, that is what the most primitive men and women had to do to survive, and nothing has really changed. Our basic instincts and needs are the same. We have evolved to do many things with our resources on our planet, but for the most part, we have kept our basic instincts. If you think about it, most mammals on earth have these basic instincts. I just wish I could teach my dogs to go make some money too and contribute toward their household.

Every day we all must basically do the same thing. It does not matter what country we live in or how primitive or advanced the country is. We all do the same thing day in and day out: how we gather our food, the shelters we live in, the method of travel we use (walking, horse, bicycle, motorcycle, car, boat, or airplane), the food we eat, relationships, and currency for trading for items. The cultures may be different, but we all must do some form of this to survive. So that means that every day, everywhere around the world, all the human beings are basically doing the same thing. Think about how many people there are on planet Earth. Now think about how many mammals there are on planet Earth. Whether you live in the African jungle or the Amazon rainforest or in Tokyo, Japan, or New York, your needs are basically the same every day. The only difference is how you are going to go about getting what you need to survive. This is true, and if you think about it, you will see that this is how the world works. So that means that if you know this, you can keep your life simple. For some reason, we have made so much confusion in our brains and our lives, haven't we? Life has become so complex for us. We all must do the same thing every day to survive, but we have made it such a complex process. Now all you have to do to simplify your life is to change your perspective into simplifying all this complexity. I call it, "Keep it simple, stupid."

Relationships, love, and sex are three things that will always be in your life. Just like positive thinking, money, exercise, and eating right, relationships are something in our lives that are always changing and that we are always working on improving. Relationships are a huge part of being a positive person and having a positive attitude, as well as being a successful and happy person. Think about it, if someone is in your life and especially if you live with them, you have another person to think about day in and day out. You have someone else to consider in most of the decisions you make day in and day out. How important is it to keep your personal relationships with a boyfriend, girlfriend, husband, or wife positive? It is a huge part of having a positive attitude. And if you are not in a relationship now, chances are you will be someday. Now throw children into this equation and you have a lot to think about and to be working on every day.

I am going to take a somewhat different approach in this chapter about relationships than most relationship books do. I have read relationship books, and I will read more in my lifetime. I enjoy relationship books very much and suggest you read some. I have been to seminars on relationships also. There is so much you can learn about relationships in books and seminars. I am going to talk about some of those things, but the main thing I am going to talk about is how a relationship can affect having a positive attitude, which you now know will affect every aspect of your life. That means that your relationships can affect every aspect of your life. As I talk about relationships in this chapter, remember one saying: "It is better to have loved and lost than to never have loved at all." Also remember that there is not much of a better life than when you are in a happy relationship. We all have the innate desire to be with a mate.

Relationships belong in this book because if you are in a relationship or when you get into a relationship someday and have a good relationship and are in love and are happy, it will help you become a truly positive, successful, happy person. If you are in a relationship and are unhappy or miserable, it will cause you to think negative thoughts, have negative feelings of unhappiness, sadness, and many others, which are all negative. It is vital to have positive, happy, loving relationships if you are going to be in a relationship. Remember this for the rest of your life. From this day forward, you need to tell yourself that you are going to be in positive, loving, happy relationships. Tell yourself that you deserve to be in these types of relationships and that you will not tolerate being in any other kind of relationship. Now put the book down and write this down on your piece of paper that you read every day: "I will make my relationship positive, happy, and loving. I will not tolerate being in bad relationships, and I will not stay in bad relationships." One of the main points that I am going to talk about in this chapter, which may not be discussed in other relationship books, is that if you are in a relationship that you do not want to be in, get out of it!

What are some things that you can do to make your life and your relationship and your attitude more positive? When we first meet someone, everything is new and exciting, and then as the years go by, everything changes. Most people and relationship books say, "Why should things change from when we first meet?" My answer to that question is, "Things change because it is just the way life is." We are always changing, so why wouldn't our relationships be changing as well? They could never stay the same years later as when we first meet someone. I believe that is one of the first things to remember if you are in a relationship. This is one of the most important things you need to learn in your life. Things are always changing in our lives. We are always changing. The world is always changing. Think about how different the world is now compared to just fifty years ago. Your relationships must change as years go by also. You must be prepared for change in all aspects of your life. Being a truly positive person will make you look forward to change. Being a negative person will make you dislike change. If you think negative thoughts all the time and are in a relationship and do not like your life and do not like yourself, your chances of having a happy, loving, positive relationship are almost impossible. Learn to embrace changes in your relationships.

"Consistency is the hobgoblin of dull minds and relationships." As years go by in your relationships, you are going to have to learn to change with them. Think about what happened at the beginning of every relationship you have ever been in. I am talking about a real relationship, when you fell in love and wanted to spend all your time with someone. You always had a goal, didn't you? When you first met someone and started thinking about them all the time, what was the next step? You had to spend time finding out if you had things in common. Your goal was to find out if you were compatible. As time went on, you began to fall in love. Then, after you fell in love, your goal was to find out if the other person fell in love with you. Then after being in love with each other, you had to find out if you wanted to have children with this person. Then you had to find out if you were compatible to live together. Your goal was to see if you could build a life with this person. Then after you moved in together, your goal was to find out if you could spend the rest of your lives together. Then you had to find out if you would want to be married to this person and if they were the person you were looking for. After all this, you may have had a goal to become engaged, planned a wedding, gotten married, and had children. All these goals were done either individually or as a couple. You had many goals in your relationship at the beginning, didn't you? After you got married and had children, did you keep setting goals for yourself and with your mate? If you did not get married or have children, have you set goals for your relationship after years have gone by? If not, why did you stop? "Consistency is the hobgoblin of dull minds and relationships." That is why our relationships become boring as they get older. We make them boring and unfulfilled by doing the same thing day in and day out, year in and year out, and not having goals as a couple. We may have individual goals, but we stop having goals as a couple, don't we?

Someone once told me, "You feel comfortable when you are with someone for a long time." This is not true. "Comfortable" is a bad word in a relationship. You should have felt comfortable with your mate early in the relationship, not years later. You should spend your life in your relationships being happy, alive, setting goals, and being positive, not comfortable. One of the first things that you need to start doing in your relationship if you are not already doing so is goal setting. Setting goals in a relationship is something that most people do not think about but is one of the most important aspects of a relationship. That is what makes a new relationship so exciting. It is the goals that you set for yourself in the relationship to find out what the other person is like and the excitement of what will happen while achieving each goal along the way. There is excitement at the beginning of a relationship to see if the goals set along the way can even be achieved. Why would you stop setting goals? Maybe it is because you did not realize that you were setting goals in the beginning of your relationship with your mate.

Every year, around New Year's Eve, I sit down with my wife and we write down our goals. I write down what my personal and business goals are for the following year, and she writes down hers, and then we write down what our goals are as a couple. I will talk more about personal and business goals in later chapters. We always include being happy and being in love in our goals, but we also take time to think about what we would like to do as a couple, what things we would like to have, what trips we would like to go on in the following year, what things we would like to change about our lives. We have done this for many years, and every December now we start talking about when we are going to write our goals down for the following year. We look forward to it. We start talking about it much before it is time to do it, so we do not forget to do it. We sit down, take a piece of paper out, and brainstorm, but usually we have already been thinking about it for about a month because we have been doing it for so long now. We are programmed as a couple to start thinking about our goals as a couple when December comes. As we sit together with our paper and pen out, we talk about what we would like to do the following year as a couple. Every year it is a little different. This proves that our goals change, and we change as people every year. What we want the current year is always different than what we want the following year. It is important for couples to know what they want. Once we are done writing our goals down on paper, we immediately go into our bathroom and tape our goals to our bathroom mirror. Recently, we put our goals in a picture frame, which is hung on the wall next to our bathroom mirror. We take our goals from our heads to paper, and then we keep them in front of us throughout the year and look at them every day to reinforce that they are important in our lives and that we will achieve them. Always tape your goals to your bathroom mirror so they are the first thing you see when you wake up and the last thing you see when you go to sleep. When we are done hanging our goals up, we always feel good, happy, positive, and excited to begin the new year as a couple. Do you see how powerful this exercise is to a relationship? How many positive things come from sitting down for one hour each year at the end of the year and making goals as a couple for the following year, then hanging them up on your bathroom mirror? It basically keeps our relationship like a new relationship.

Every relationship book and every couple that you talk to that has been together for many years will tell you that the secret to a lasting relationship is communication and not letting the relationship get stale. There are other things that they will talk about, but they will always have those two things in common, no matter who you talk with. I have read relationship books, and I always go out of my way to ask people what the secret to a long relationship is a person or couple tells me they have been together fifteen, twenty, twenty-five years. When you set goals as a couple every year, you are accomplishing both, aren't you? When you set goals as a couple, you will see that something very special will happen. You will see that your mate will know that you are serious about your relationship. If you let someone look at your list that you have made to read every day, I bet they would say you are serious about becoming a positive thinker. When couples have goals and they are clear and defined and written down, their relationship becomes fresh every year and by setting goals together both people realize that they are a strong couple going into a new year with goals that they have set together.

At first when you suggest to your mate that you should both sit down and write down goals, they will look at you like you are crazy. People are just not used to doing things like this, and I can guarantee you that your mate has never done this with someone in a relationship. What you should do is bring it up to your mate right away. Do not wait for the end of the year. Do it now. You can write down goals for the rest of whatever year you are reading this book. If it is near the end of the year, then just make your list for next year now and then do your goals at the end of the following year. The most important thing is that you do it now while the idea seems right to you. If you wait after reading this chapter, the chances are that you will not bring it up if time goes by. If you sit down now with your mate and make goals with your mate, you will set the basis for the rest of your relationship. My suggestion to you is that you tell your mate that you read something interesting in this book about relationships and it made sense. Then take a couple of days to think about some things that you would like to do as a couple in the future. Do not wait too long to sit down and put your goals as a couple on paper. Explain to your mate how the goals work and that you believe it will improve your relationship and keep it fresh. Do not get upset if your mate thinks you are crazy when you bring this up. People are not used to ideas like this. Once you sit down and start putting some things on paper and talking about what you would like to both do as a couple, you will see that it is fun and exciting. Do not be afraid to add some things to the list as the weeks go by. But the most important thing is to put something down on the list of goals. Put a title on the paper: "Our Goals." Then it is very important to tape the list to your bathroom mirror. Again, your mate will probably think you are crazy. It is OK—you are not crazy. This is what happy, positive, successful people do. It is not crazy. You must put your list somewhere that will force you to look at it every day when you wake up and before you go to bed.

As time goes by and you look at your goals every day, you will see that looking at the list will make you feel better about your relationship, and you will be happy that you now have some goals as to what you and your mate want to do as a couple. Have you ever heard couples say, "We are drifting apart" or "We just drifted apart"? Why do you think that is? Now you know the answer. It is because when people first meet, they have goals. They are drifting together. And as the years go by, if they do not keep making goals as a couple, they start to drift apart. It is such a simple thing, but such a huge thing to guard against in a relationship.

When you drift apart from your mate, you can fall into a deep, negative hole. No matter how positive of a person you are, your relationships are always on your mind. If you live with someone, then that person is in your life twenty-four hours a day, seven days a week. There are some things in relationships that can become completely negative. Now we have eliminated one of them—drifting apart. When you grow as a couple together, you will see that you have the secret to a happy, positive relationship. Will life throw things at you and your mate as a couple? You better believe it. But as you are growing together, by having goals as a couple, you can now overcome them together, the same way you will overcome negative things by yourself. This will make your positive world a much better one. When we are happy in our relationships, we are happier overall.

If you are in a relationship, who are you going to spend most of your time with? You are going to spend most of your time when you are not at work with your mate. What kind of conversations do you have when you are with your mate? Are they positive? Do you ever talk about other people? Of course, you do. Do you talk about other people in a positive manner? Remember that when you are with your mate, it is even more important to talk about positive things and to talk about people in a positive way. Having positive conversations with your mate is one of the most important things you are going to have to do to be a truly positive person. So how are you going to change your conversations if you are used to having negative conversations with your mate? The first thing to remember is that when you talk negatively with your mate, you will be telling your subconscious that it is OK to be negative. How can you achieve a positive attitude when you are having negative conversations with the most important person in your life? You cannot. I wish I could say that it can work, but it cannot. There are two things that you must change immediately while talking with your spouse. The first thing is to make sure you do not talk about other people in a negative manner. That means your family, your friends, the people you work with, and everyone else that you talk about. The second thing is not to talk negatively about your mate. Always tell the truth, but do not be negative. Always try to be positive while talking to your mate about them. Do not be fake. Always be genuine, but do not be negative. Now if you do this, what other chances do you have to speak negatively with your mate? There are none, right? If you do just two things, you will always have positive conversations with your mate.

Here is how you can achieve always having positive conversations with your mate. The first step is to realize that this will not happen overnight and that you must practice this. You will have to be patient and know that you will make mistakes at first. If you find yourself getting into a negative conversation about someone with your spouse, do not freak out. It is going to happen. I do it all the time. I am not perfect. But I always identify it right away and turn the conversation into a positive one. I always find the positive in people. The first step is to just pay attention to your conversations with your mate. You will probably be shocked at how negative your conversations are. For some reason, it makes people feel better to talk negatively about people, so they think. What they do not realize is that nothing could be farther from the truth. Do you understand? If you do not, you will once you start paying attention to the difference in the way you feel when you have positive conversations with your spouse instead of negative ones. This is step one. Be patient, and start practicing having positive conversations with your mate. The conversations will most likely turn back to being negative, but then say positive things and watch what happens. After a while, your mate will automatically engage in positive conversations with you, but you are now the leader in these conversations. You are the coach. You do not have to say anything. Just say positive things in your conversations. And whatever you do, do not get upset if your mate is not engaging in positive conversations as fast as you want them to. Remember, they have spent a lifetime programming themselves to be who they are. But when you get good at turning negative conversations into positive ones with your mate, they will start understanding.

Never get upset because you are ahead of your spouse in being a positive person. Once you begin to become positive, it will be hard and frustrating to have negative conversations with your mate. Take time to let your relationship become positive. Work on it every day as you work on your own positive relationship with yourself. Always remember to enjoy the journey and to remember that this is a marathon, not a sprint. You will be in relationships for the rest of your life.

Another way for you to have positive conversations with your mate is to practice this one technique when you leave a friend's house or a party or a social gathering with people you know. What do couples usually do when they leave a party or a get-together at a friend's house? They get in the car and immediately start talking negatively about all the people they were just with. This is one of the most negative things that a couple can do together. The only more negative thing is for a couple to speak negatively about each other.

When you get in the car to leave from a party or social get-together with friends, coworkers, soccer moms and dads, or from your family's house, do not engage in negative talk about the people you were just with. Instead, find the positive things that you saw in the people. Talk about how cute their children were, how they lost weight, or how good or happy some of them looked. Do not find negative things to talk about while you are driving home from being with people you know. The easiest way to do this is to have positive conversations with the people while you are at a social or family event. Then you should have many positive things to talk about. But even if you do have positive conversations, you are going to remember to have positive conversations when you are alone with your mate also.

Another way that this book is going to be different from a relationship book is that I firmly believe that if you are not happy in a relationship, you should get out of it. This is plain and simple. If you are not happy, leave. I see so many people in my lifetime stay in relationships when they are unhappy. I know that they are not going to stay together, and no matter how long it takes, they always separate or get divorced. They know they do not want to be together, but they stay together for a variety of reasons. They either do not want to take the time to separate, are afraid of the financial consequences of separating, are afraid of being alone, as well as other reasons. If you know that you are not in love any longer and you know that you do not want to spend the rest of your life with someone, then why would you want to stay in the relationship? This is very negative and will weigh on you in a negative manner. You can try to push it deep down in your mind and not feel the pain and unhappiness it will cause you, but eventually it will not work any longer, and then you will just wake up one day and tell yourself you are done. Why wait to go through this entire process before you leave a relationship? To say that you have tried. I believe that when you become truly positive and you learn to follow your gut and God, you will not want to wait around in bad relationships until it is time to end it. If you know you are not in love any longer, it is time to get out now.

I am not talking about relationships that you may be in where it is clear to yourself that you are not in it to be in love and to be married or to move in together and possibly spend the rest of your lives together. When you are in relationships that are not serious and you and the other person know where you stand, there is no reason to overanalyze it. But when you have fallen in love with someone, moved in together, and maybe gotten married and that changes to arguing all the time, not liking each other, and not being in love any longer, it is time to leave. Leaving a relationship that you know is over or a relationship in which you know that you are not in love with someone any longer can be a very positive thing in your life. Staying in these relationships can be a very negative thing in your life. If you stay in relationships that are negative, your entire life will change. It will weigh on you as years go by, like an elephant sitting on your shoulders. I have been in relationships with very nice, smart, beautiful women. There was nothing wrong with them, and I am sure that they are very happy now. We were just not right together. You must tell yourself this when you are in bad relationships. People make so many excuses when a relationship ends about why it did not work out. They say things like "He or she was crazy" or "They were an alcoholic" or "They were screwed up as a child." Very few people just say, "We were not right for each other." Usually, that is the case. I can tell you that all my relationships in my life ended because we were not right for each other. I have had relationships where the woman I was with realized that I was not right for her, and she ended it. When I was younger, I was guilty of saying these crazy things when I would end a relationship with a woman, but I learned not to say those things. I realized that it is very negative. Again, it is OK to speak the truth and how you feel about someone when you leave a relationship, but if you think about it, most of your relationships in your lifetime ended because you were not right for each other and one of you or both of you figured that out at some point.

When we stay in negative relationships, so many bad things will happen to us. As human beings, we are naturally drawn to being with a mate. That is what humans do. We find a mate, and then we build a life together. Don't worry if you are single and happy, congratulations to you. You should not worry about anything, and you should be very happy that you like your life. But most people either are in a relationship or would like to be in one. If you think about it, there is really nothing much more negative and emotionally draining than when you are in a bad relationship. You will release so many bad chemicals into your body when you are in a bad relationship. It is exactly the opposite of how incredible you feel when you first meet someone and fall in love. The world is a wonderful place when you first meet someone and fall in love, isn't it? I have also talked with people that have been together or married for fifteen, twenty, and thirty years, and they are the happiest they have ever been since the day they met. But when you are with someone and you are unhappy day in and day out and you do not want to go home to see them after work or you do not want to look at them or talk to them any longer, it might be time to end it. Listen to your heart, to your head, and to your gut. They will not lie to you.

I am not saying that if you are in a bad relationship or if your relationship becomes bad suddenly, you should leave. I am telling you that if you know in your heart and in your mind that you do not want to be with someone any longer or if you know you are not in love any longer, then do not prolong the inevitable. Staying in relationships that you know you do not want to be in, or you should not be in is an extremely negative thing. If you know in your heart that you still are in love with someone and they are telling you that they are in love with you, then it is very positive to work through hard times in relationships. There is nothing more rewarding and positive than working through hard times with someone you love. Life gets in the way, and people change in relationships. They are not always easy, and they require a lot of work. This is what you will read in relationship books and hear in relationship seminars. It is always positive to work at a relationship and to try to stay in a relationship that you think is worth being in. Even if you are arguing with your mate or you are not happy, but you know that the right thing to do is to stay in the relationship and try to make it right, always consider this a positive thing that you are doing. Relationships are worth fighting for, and you will have different challenges with someone else if you get into another relationship. But when you know in your heart that it is time to get out of a relationship, save your time and protect your positive attitude.

When you are in a relationship and try to think positive thoughts and say positive things, you will find that as you learn how to become more positive, your mate may fall behind you in being positive. Do not begin to get upset if this happens. If you are spending time to become positive and learning how to become truly positive and your mate is not, you may begin to grow apart. They will be in one place mentally, and you will be in another. I have had that happen to me when I was in my early twenties. My suggestion to you is to introduce positive things into your relationship right away. It is time to put the book down again and get the piece of paper that you look at every day and every night. Write down, "I will be patient in my relationship while becoming truly positive, and I will introduce positive things into my relationship right away. I will make it a goal to attend positive functions with my mate, and we will become positive people together." Now is the time to find ways to do more things that you and your mate consider positive things in your life. Remember that you are the leader now in being positive in your relationship. Take the time to find out what your mate likes in life and considers positive. Do not engage in negative talk with your mate, and do not have negative conversations about people with your mate. If your mate notices that you are not having the same conversations that you used to have, explain that you are going to make your life and your lives better by being positive. Your mate will understand after a while what you are doing. Everyone knows the difference between being positive and being negative, and nine out of ten people would much rather be positive than negative. They just do not know how. The chances are that your mate will embrace the fact that you are making a change for the better in your life and in your relationship. But they will only respond to you once they see that you are in this for the long haul and that it is not a passing phase. When your mate sees time go by and you are getting more and more positive, they will naturally respond to you. Do not be surprised if your mate spends a little time observing you and making sure that you are truly committed to making a change to be a truly positive person before they respond to the new you.

CHAPTER 8

What Is It You Really Want?
Learn How to Dream

Now that you know you how your conscious mind and your subconscious mind work and you know the secret to what happy, successful, positive, even famous people and professional athletes know, you have to start learning how to dream. You also must learn how to define what you really want in life. Do you remember when you were in high school and everyone kept asking you, "What are you going to do after high school?" If you were like most teenagers, you probably wondered what you were going to do also. Even if you were going to go to college, the chances are you didn't know what you wanted to do in life or what profession you were going to get into. As you went through your twenties, you probably spent a lot of time trying to find yourself and figuring out what you wanted to do in life to make money and have a career. You probably spent a lot of time wondering if you wanted to be married or have children. If you did get married and have children, the chances are that you spent some time wondering if you made the right decision. If you are in your twenties you are probably thinking about these things. No matter how old you are now, you probably still question and wonder what your life has in store for you. I would never have thought that I would be writing a book at forty-five years old when I was in my twenties. Writing a book was the farthest thing from my mind.

One day about eight years ago, I woke up one morning and said to myself that I wanted to write a book someday. I know what happy, positive, successful people know, so once I had that eager feeling and analyzed it in my mind and listened to my gut to answer the question, "Is this something I really wanted to do?" I knew I would write a book someday, unless I decided not to. I went to an office-supply store right away and bought a small paper binder, and I started writing things down that were coming out of my head about this book. I carried it around everywhere, and if I had a thought or an idea, I wrote it down. Then one day, something happened in my life that put the book on hold. I never stopped wanting to write the book, but I knew I could not pursue it at that time. I put the small binder with my thoughts in a drawer next to my bed, and it sat there for eight years. I would see it every so often when I opened that drawer. The drawer is more of an overflow drawer and does not have clothes in it. As the years went by, sometimes I would look at the binder and smile a little, thinking about how excited I was when I decided to write a book and knowing that unless I decided not to write the book, it would be written someday.

Then one day something told me that it was time to write the book. Do you know what that something was? It was my subconscious. I never stopped thinking about writing this book from the day I decided to until eight years later. This book had a place in my brain for eight years. Think of it as kind of like being on a shelf. This book was on a shelf in my brain for eight years. I could not pursue writing this book eight years earlier because events in my life changed, and I would not have been able to enjoy writing the book. I never stopped thinking about writing the book. It was not every day, but I often thought about writing this book. The key to this is that for eight years, every time I thought about writing this book, I never ended the conversation with myself by saying, "I do not think you should write a book any longer." I never told myself that I didn't want to write a book or thought to myself that writing a book was something that sounded great and fun years ago but was something that I didn't want to pursue any longer. "Sometimes in life if you know what you don't want, it is better than knowing what you do want." In this case, as time went on, I never felt that I did not want to write the book. Every time I looked at the little binder with my thoughts in it or talked to someone about writing a book or thought to myself that I wanted to write a book, I always felt the same way afterward. I always wanted to do it.

There are five things that happened to me for me to get this book from thoughts in my head and written down in a small binder and into your hands. I had to first figure out if I wanted to write a book and then get past my fears about writing a book and then listen to my gut to wonder if it was the right thing to pursue in my life. And then once I did all that, I had to dream about it often and learn about it in order to make it a reality. I had to define exactly what kind of book I wanted to write. I knew how I wanted the cover to look and what color I wanted the book to be. I know that if I really want something and I explore all the details and take my time to figure out about something and then make a decision that I want to pursue something, all I have to do is start dreaming about it, and unless I decide for some reason that I do not want to pursue the dream any longer, it will happen for me. I also know that things will happen along the way that will get in my way, slow me down, speed me up, and change my dreams a little. I know this, so when things happen, when life happens, I do not stress out over it. I know that it is part of the process of taking a dream to a reality. Take out your piece of paper that you look at every day and write this down. "Taking a dream to a reality is a process."

Who would have ever thought that I would write a book? What I have learned and what you are going to learn is that when something sounds interesting to you and you research it and you feel in your gut that it is something you want to do and you think about it constantly (dream), you need to go get it! I have done this many times in my life, so I knew what was happening throughout the eight-year process to begin writing this book. I knew that if I decided one day, truly decided one day, that I did not want to write a book any longer, I would not be upset. I also knew that if I kept dreaming about writing a book and kept concluding with myself that it was something I was going to do, then all I had to do was dream about it. Notice I am using the word "dream." Dreaming is not just something you do when you sleep. You can dream while you are awake also. Dreaming when you are sleeping and when you are awake are not the same, but they are similar. When you dream about something, you are basically thinking about it so much that it makes you have a state of euphoria about it as time goes on. Dreaming is not thinking about something negative that makes you feel bad. It is something that makes you feel great. Or dreaming could be thinking constantly about something that you want. It could be a bicycle, a piece of jewelry, a car, furniture, a house, a plane, or a trip to somewhere you have always wanted to see. Dreaming could be about starting your own business or wanting to not ever work a day in your life again. You could dream about having a child or being married someday. Dreaming is whatever creeps into your brain and then goes into your gut, and you cannot stop thinking about it because you want it so badly.

Most people teach themselves to not dream about things. They have taught themselves that dreaming can be a letdown or can become a negative thing because if they dream about something and then do not get it time after time, it is better not to dream at all. Is this you? Is this someone you know? Remember, it's your time and it's your turn. If you do this, you are not going to any longer. If you do not do this, then you are going to learn how to master dreaming and how to get what you want in life. Not only are you going to learn how to dream, but you are going to learn how to dream big. I want you to dream and dream big. Dreaming is one of the best-kept secrets of movie stars, singers, athletes, business owners, soccer moms and dads, and on and on. Dreaming is the difference and is what those people are doing that you have been observing that are happy, positive, and successful all the time. Dreaming is why when you look at some people that are staring into space, they have a smile on their face and a gleam in their eye you can see. Dreaming is why once you become a positive person and program your subconscious to be positive, your dreams will come true. Dreaming is how you tap into the positive energy around you, around others, the planet, and the universe. Dreaming is how you get what you want or what you do not want in life. It all starts with having a positive attitude, but it ends with dreaming.

All the things in this book go together. Think of them as different functions in your body and mind that achieve one goal. Every day we have a chance to make decisions and to think in a positive or negative manner. Almost everything we do each day and each night has a positive and negative path to it. Think about this for a minute, and you will see it is true. You can look at anything in a positive or a negative way. When you are dreaming about something, there is no difference. You can tell yourself, "I am going to go get it!" Or you can tell yourself, "I will never get this." Dreaming is the same as every other technique in this book. You are going to have to do it to believe that it will happen, you are going to have to try it and see that it can happen, and you are going to have to reprogram your subconscious to believe that when you dream about something, you get what you want. You are also going to have to be patient with yourself and your dreams. You are going to have to remember that you will have dreams until the day you die. We never stop dreaming about things. You must remember that this is a marathon, not a sprint. You have spent a lifetime becoming who you are, and today is the first day of the rest of your life. You can make whatever you want to out of tomorrow.

How do we know that dreaming is real? How do we know that dreaming is something that humans do? Just look around you. Look at the house you live in. Look at what happens when you turn on a light switch. Look at what happens when you turn on a water faucet. You can turn on your stove and there is fire, or an electric burner comes on for you to cook your food. Look at a downtown of any city. Think about how tall the buildings are and what it took to build them. Think about the roads and freeways you drive on every day. Think about how people fly on an airplane from one city or country to another. Think about how many small businesses there are. You can pull your car over and buy a sandwich in five minutes, get back into your car, and then go home after work or just stay in your car and your food is given to you. Everything that humans do on earth day in and day out came from a dream. Someone came up with an idea and then researched and thought about it, in some cases for a lifetime, before their dream became a reality. A dream can also be a little thing as well. A dream can be to buy a pair of shoes or a leather jacket that you want but cannot afford. A dream can be anything. What successful, happy, positive people know is that things they want in life start with a dream.

Have you ever heard the line "The rich get richer"? It is true. Why do the rich get richer? They get richer because they dream bigger and bigger, and they do not stop dreaming and achieving when they reach one goal. They keep dreaming bigger. That is right. You can dream, achieve that dream, and then dream bigger. It is like stepping-stones. It is like walking upstairs until you get to the top of where you are going. Dreaming can be so huge and complex that you will have to achieve your dream in phases. How did the ancient Egyptians build the pyramids? We are still not sure. Someone must have had a dream to build a structure that high, in that shape, in the place they built it, and meant it as a symbol of their society. I bet someone spent many years thinking about exactly how they wanted the pyramids to look before they started building them. They had to assemble a team of people to analyze their dream and to tell them if and how it could be achieved. They might have had to make changes to their dream along the way in order to achieve it. But the pyramids did come from a dream. They surely did not appear overnight. They appeared over many, many years and are still standing today. The rich just don't get richer; they make that happen. People that are extremely happy and successful are not just born this way. They are not just lucky. They dream about becoming who they are. They program their subconscious through thoughts of who they want to be and what things they want, and then they go get it! This is the formula to success. This is the secret to the world. It is putting thought into action and then believing that you can achieve whatever you set your mind to. It's not a fantasy, it's not made believe and it's not something that just other people do.

It's something that you are going to learn to do and to achieve. Dreaming is will become your best friend and make you feel good and excited, not scared and depressed.

When you dream and set your mind to something, you will surely have it. How does this happen? It happens because every day windows are opening and closing in front of you. Every day there are paths in front of us to take. Every day there are decisions to make, all which lead to different results in our lives. Every day there are people in our lives that we interact with that can affect our lives in positive and negative ways. How we interact with them will alter their opinions of us, which will alter the way they perceive us, which will alter the way they interact with us. Every day we attract positive or negative energy around us, which will affect the outcome of our day, our week, our month, or our year. Not every day is such a dramatic event. Some days are dull and boring, and not much happens. But some days all this happens. The only question is, when this does happen, are you ready to make the most of it? Are you ready to take advantage of it? Do you even believe that this all can happen for you? Movie stars, athletes, singers, entrepreneurs, moms and dads, supervisors, scientists, and positive people all around the world believe it can. They also believe that they deserve for it to happen to them. They take their dreams, and they turn them into reality by thinking positive thoughts about their dreams constantly and by programming their subconscious to know that when they dream, it will become a reality, unless they decide not to make it happen. They are open to the positive energy and the correct paths that they face each day. They embrace and relish all this every day. Whether they are a lion or a gazelle, when the sun comes up, they are running after their dreams.

What successful people also know is that everything does not go perfectly while achieving their dreams. There are always obstacles and setbacks along the way. There are professional athletes that have suffered serious injuries, only to overcome them and go on to be superstars. There are singers that have been told early on in their careers that they will never make it in the music industry that have gone on to become icons of their industry and are among the top record sellers. There are actors and actresses that have been told that they will never make it in the movie industry that now make $20 million per movie and love their craft and are respected among the highest achievers of their craft. There are people that have built a company and then lost everything, filed bankruptcy, only to rebuild another company and are now multimillionaires and doing what they love. There are husbands and wives, moms and dads that have had challenges with their children and with their lives, and now their children are successful doctors, lawyers, and CEOs. There are people that have worked their way up to a position in their company that makes them wake up every day and love going to work. There are people that were members of gangs that had no hope of living a normal life that now run their own youth organizations to help children become better adults. This list goes on and on. From the top of the ladder to the bottom, there is no better dream. There is only a dream. Every dream is a great dream, no matter how big or small. That is what makes us unique. That is what makes us human.

Now let's learn how to make all this happen. Remember that everything in this book is related. The first thing you must do is define what you want. "You must first discover what you want, and then go get it." Maybe you already know what you want. Maybe you do not want anything right now. It does not matter. Nothing matters except what you want out of life. Remember this; it is important. If you do not have any dreams right now, there is nothing wrong with that. Do not make a dream up. Just relax, and enjoy what you have right now. But if you do have a dream or when you do have a dream, this is all you have to do to achieve it. You always must keep that dream in front of you. You must think about it all day and all night. By "all day and all night" I do not mean that you do not think about anything else or do anything else. You do all your normal activities every day, but you always keep your dream in front of you. So how do you this? You must always be thinking about your dream. You always must be able to see your dream in your head. Your dream must be clearly defined in your head. You must be able to talk about your dream at any moment and recite every time exactly what your dream is about. You should know every detail of your dream: sizes, colors, smells, how it looks, how it feels, how it functions, what it will take to achieve your dream—exactly what it will take to achieve your dream. Your dreams must be very well defined, and they should be achievable. You should also dream big. Learn to think big and to dream big!

After you define your dream and you know 100 percent that you are going to achieve your dream, believe in your body, your mind, and your soul that you are going to achieve it. Feel your dream in your body. When you get excited about your dream, never ever suppress that feeling and never think negative thoughts about your dream. Look at challenges in achieving your dream as positive obstacles, and know that challenges are just part of achieving a dream. Challenges are not negative; they are positive. "Anything worth achieving is worth fighting for." Write this down on the piece of paper that you look at every day. Then once you do all this, you must take your dream out of your head and put it on paper to make it real. How do you think you do this? Simple, you write it down on your personal goals that you write down every year around New Year's Eve. If you start dreaming about something and decide you are going to go for that dream, then write it down on your list of goals immediately. Do not wait until the end of the year. Your goals are just that, yours, and you can add to them anytime you want to. I will sometimes add a goal or two and take off a goal or two throughout the year. Sometimes if I achieve a goal that I have put on my list of goals early in the year, I will also keep it on my list to remind me that I have achieved it and to reinforce the fact that I am a goal achiever. This is what happy, positive, successful people know that everyone else does not. They have learned to write their dreams down and keep them in front of them every day to confirm that they are going to achieve them.

Think of the lists that you are developing while reading this book as a "personal life plan" and a "personal business plan." This all may seem completely crazy to you right now. This may sound like science fiction. It may sound ridiculous and stupid. It may even sound like it will not work for you. I can assure you that this works. All of it. Every technique in this book works. Not only does it all work, but it all goes together to reinforce each technique and enhance the total package of happiness, success and achieving a positive attitude. The only reason you may not have heard of this before in your lifetime is because you have never taken the time to learn about it or no one has shown you, but more so, there is not a lot of learning material on this subject. And people that know these secrets and techniques are busy achieving their goals and living their lives, so they do not have time to share what they know. Every successful large corporation has a business plan. Every time I have applied for a loan on my office building, I have had to show them a business plan for my companies. It had to be completely detailed and took weeks to prepare. Not only did I have to prepare a business plan, but the bank doing my loans would always call me weeks later after I submitted my business plans to discuss my business plans with me and make sure I was on the right track. My business plans were the same as everything I am describing in these chapters. They talked about where I was going the first year, second year, and many years from the day I wrote the plans. I talked about how many employees I would have. I talked about how much money my goal was to make each year. I talked about what the culture of the company would be like. Because I was the sole owner of the building I was buying and refinancing and the sole owner of the businesses, my business plans were also part of my personal plans, my dreams. But the thing to remember here is that a bank requested to see these dreams and goals. They are called a business plan, but they were just dreams and goals of mine put down and translated to numbers and words. For me it was simple to whip out a business plan. I had it written down, and it was in my head, right in front of me, every day. This is all real. It does exist. Think of it as a secret society that you are now part of. If you must do some of this for your job, then just take it to the next level and do it for your personal life also. They all go together. It all goes together. If you have never done any of this, then welcome to the party, buckle up for a wild ride because it's your time and it's your turn.

Every large corporation and successful family do some form of dreaming, goal achieving, and most importantly, positive thinking. Some corporations study what colors to paint the walls in their offices to make their employees the happiest. Some companies require their employees to decorate their workspace with balloons, pictures, banners, and whatever they want to. Most corporations know exactly where they are headed every quarter and spend a lot of time to analyze where they are at all times. Some large corporations do not work on a yearly business plan at all. They work on monthly reports or quarterly reports. Some large corporations work off weekly business plans. The thing that they all have in common is that they all work off business plans, and business plans are nothing more than goals and dreams that went from someone's head onto a piece of paper. That is how a business plan starts. The execution of a business plan may be extremely complex and require many people and many things to achieve, but how the business plan became written is always the same. Now that you know this, why wouldn't you make a business plan of your own? Why wouldn't you always have a personal plan of your own written down? It is time for you to pull the curtain back on success, happiness, and positivity. Think of it like going backstage at a magic show and seeing how the magician has done his tricks and illusions. The reason you should be practicing these techniques is because they work. If they did not, I would not have had to submit a business plan to refinance an office building to a bank. Do a business plan and a refinance on an office building go together? At first it sounds ridiculous, doesn't it? But it is how the bank got to know me and what my business goals were. By making me write them down and send them to them, they could determine if I was going to be able to pay them back every month. If I could not produce one or if I did not know how to make a business plan, then how could I have a successful business? Why do you think around 60 percent of businesses fail within the first five years? There are other reasons, but not having a clear, attainable business plan is very high on the list of reasons. I believe that another big reason people fail at opening a business is because they do not know how to think positively, and when they experience challenges, their negative thoughts and programming get the best of them. I believe that a large percentage of the 60 percent that fail every year are not programmed to be successful. But the awesome thing about business and humans is that even if you fail, you can come back to try again. And because you have tried and failed and come back again, you have taken a huge step in reprogramming yourself to never quit.

Everyone wants to be an entrepreneur, but they don't want to do the work to do it when they find out how much work it is. "Whatever you believe you will achieve." "You have to feed your own ego all the time so you can be what you want to be." "If you don't take risks, how can you change the world?" "Realize that everyone has doubts and fears, not just you. It's what you do about them and how you handle them that counts." "Don't let age stand in your way." "You have to be a problem solver." "Show me a good loser, and I will show you a loser." "You have to believe you are the best, but it doesn't mean you are better." "Part-time effort will result in part-time results." These are just a few saying out of hundreds that people have made up about being positive, happy, and successful. Some of those are my own sayings. Why do you think there are sayings like this? It is because they are true, and people have taken the time to write them down so they can remember them, live by them, and use them. Write your own sayings down. Add to the list that you look at every day and night. Make it your own as time goes by. Use your lists and goals as a map to get to where you want to go in your life.

Once you begin to practice all these techniques and reprogram your mind, something is going to happen. You are going to experience emotions that may make you want to stop practicing the techniques. Some of these emotions are fear, doubt, tiredness, uncertainty confusion, and negativity toward the techniques. You may also find yourself talking yourself out of believing that they will work for you or that they work at all. This is your subconscious talking to you. It is programmed to not let you get hurt and not be positive and happy all the time. It is programmed not to take risks and to protect you from feeling anxiety over failure and that you are not as good as others. Your subconscious may have been programmed not to dream and not to take risks. It may try to stop you early on. You have most likely always had this inner battle when you have thought about stepping out of your comfort zone or taking a risk.

The good news for you is that everyone is like this. I am not different. I am always afraid when I take a risk or step out of my comfort zone. Everyone I have ever known is the same way. You are going to have to learn how to overcome fear, anxiety, and how to step out of your comfort zone. And the fantastic news is that you can change your fears and anxieties about failure and dreaming around easily.

When you have a dream, just know that there will be obstacles along the way. But before you put a dream into action by defining it and writing it down, you are going to have to overcome the initial fears of telling yourself that you are going to move forward with your dream. Taking a dream from an idea in your head to a plan of action that you begin to make a reality is kind of like stepping to the edge of a very high cliff with water at the bottom and contemplating jumping off and then doing it. If you were standing at the edge of a very high cliff, looking at water at the bottom and contemplating jumping, what would be going through your head? You would be thinking about whether you were going to get hurt, if you were capable of making a jump like that, if the cliff was too high, if the water was deep enough, if you could jump out far enough to miss the rocks at the bottom of the cliff. All these things and many more would be going through your head very quickly. You would not have to think about these things. They would already be built into your brain, and they would be pouring out into your thoughts. You would be having a conversation with yourself as to whether or not you should jump and what would happen if you did. There would also be one major emotion that you would have to overcome. That emotion is fear. If you could not overcome the fear of jumping and what would happen, you would never jump. Then surely someone else would walk up to the edge of that cliff, stand there, and jump off it, only to splash out of the water with a loud scream of joy, exhilaration, and accomplishment. Having a dream is no different. You are jumping off a cliff. You are doing something you have never done before. It is new territory. Why do you think thrill seekers are so addicted to thrills? They love the unknown. They love the sense of achievement they get. They enjoy overcoming their fears.

When you have a dream and you feel that fear creep up into your mind and your stomach, know it is perfectly normal. It is your subconscious slowing you down and telling you, "Are you sure you should do this?" Just like what would happen if you were standing on a very high cliff, looking down at water. There are real consequences to failing at a dream. But guess what? If you never take risks, you will never achieve anything new. If humans never took risks, we would still be living in caves, making fires at night, and hunting animals to eat. Everything on planet Earth that humans have achieved started with a dream and a risk. And then whoever had that dream had to jump off the cliff into the water and make it happen. "The more dreams and risks a person make in their lives, the more dreams they will achieve". When you have a dream and you feel that little twinge of fear and doubt, relish in it. When you get to the point while dreaming that you feel fear and doubt, that means that your subconscious knows you are serious about it. Take time to analyze your fears and doubts. But here is the secret to overcoming them. Listen to your gut. That is right. Literally listen to how your stomach is feeling. Listen to your body, and listen to your mind. Take the time to analyze all the emotions you are feeling. They are there for a reason. But tell yourself right now and whenever you begin to dream that you are not going to let fear stand in the way of what you want. Put the book down for a few minutes and close your eyes now. Tell yourself that you are not going to let fear stand in the way of your dreaming and having what you want in life any longer. Smile in your brain and with your mouth. Tell yourself that you are proud of yourself for learning this technique of how to overcome your fears while dreaming and setting goals for your life. Take a deep breath, and relax while thinking positive thoughts about how much different your life is now going to be because you now know some of the keys to success, happiness, and being positive. Give yourself a mental pat on the back, and tell yourself that you are going to read more books, go to seminars, and learn more about these techniques and that you are going to learn more techniques on how to dream, achieve your goals, and overcome your fears. Do it now.

Write down on that piece of paper that you look at every day and night that you are not going to let your fears get in the way of your dreams. When you feel that feeling in your gut and your mind is telling you to slow down and analyze your dream, listen to it. But just know that your conscious mind has the ultimate decision as to whether you are going to move past your fears and make your dream a reality. Take as much time as you need to analyze your dream before you put it into action and begin to make it a reality. Look at all the good things you can think of and all the bad things. Listen to your gut while you are thinking about turning a dream into a reality. If you conclude that you want to turn your dream into a reality, then here is the single most important thing that you must do and remember every time! When you decide to turn a dream into a reality, you must tell yourself that you are going to go for it and never look back. You must always think of moving forward with your dream and never look back. You must decide to achieve what you believe. You must, at that moment, let your fears go and believe in yourself. From the moment you decide to follow your gut because you have analyzed your dream and taken the time to know it is something you want to do; you must let your fears go. Do not accept fear any longer in the conversation you have with yourself about your dream after you decide to achieve it. Consider fear at that point as a negative emotion, and do not tolerate it. Fear is no longer part of the equation for you to achieve your dream. The only time fear is tolerated and accepted during determining whether you want to pursue a dream is while you are analyzing all the aspects of the dream before you decide to achieve it. This is what truly happy, successful, positive people know and practice.

While you are achieving your dreams, you will need to follow your gut and overcome your fears along the way. All successful people know and experience this. If you have a dream that will take years to achieve, you will have to overcome obstacles, fears, and follow your gut while making decisions for years. This is normal and happens to everyone. Know that this is not just happening to you. We all go through this process while achieving our dreams. Things will challenge your dream, and obstacles will pop up along the way that you did not account for while first making your decision to achieve your dream. This is all right. It happens to everyone. It is part of achieving a dream. We do not live in a perfect world, remember? If you could just think of a dream and it magically appeared, it would not be a dream. It would be a singular thought. A dream is many thoughts and many actions put into motion to achieve a single or group of goals. A dream is what you make of it. A dream is a journey that you get to go on with yourself.

Now that you know the secrets to dreaming and to getting what you want in life, start dreaming! Do not hold back. Give yourself some time to learn how to dream again. We all knew how to dream when we were children and teenagers. Some of us chose to stop ourselves from dreaming though and told ourselves that we were not worthy of dreaming and that dreaming can cause pain and be a negative thing. Learn to dream again! Learn to dream big! Learn to follow your dreams! Learn to achieve your dreams! Tell yourself that you deserve to have dreams and that you deserve to achieve your dreams. Tell yourself that you are not going to let fear and negativity stop you from dreaming. Ask God to help you with your dreams and to guide you in making the right decisions while dreaming. While you are dreaming, know that whatever happens, if you decide to turn a dream into reality, it is meant to be. Something good comes out of every adventure in your life. If you decide not to pursue a dream, know that it is meant to be and do not dwell on your decision. There are no wrong decisions. Something good will come out of everything you do in life. All you have to do is take the time to figure out what good came from it. When you dream, trust yourself. Believe in yourself. Make your dreams your reality. "Every thought kept ever constant leads to action and results follow thoughts which determine what you want. Action determines what you get, and action is thought in motion." Write this down on your piece of paper that you look at every day and every night.

Now that you are going to figure out what you want and you know how to get it, there is something else that you are going to have to do. You need to put things that you want in front of you at all times. How do you do this? There is a technique that will help you get what you dream about. Let's say that you want a red sports car and you know exactly what make and model you want. You know what type of interior you want and what shade of red. You know the kind of wheels and tires you want on it, and you know if you want the windows tinted and how dark you want them tinted. You may know exactly what kind of options you want on the car. Now there are only two things left that you must do to get this car someday. Number one is that you must go drive it. You must sit in it, smell it, see it up close and in person. You must listen to the way the car sounds when you start it. You must look at all the details of the car and learn about the car and what it is you like about it. Then after you see and drive the car, you have to get a picture of the car and hang it up in your kitchen, in your office, or somewhere in your house that will make you look at it every day. What this will do is make you visualize yourself owning and driving that car every day. Once you know that you have driven the car and decide that you want it, then all you have to do is visualize it. Once you visualize having something and look at it repeatedly day in and day out, it is yours. Your mind and your subconscious will find a way to get it. You will attract positive energy that will help you get what you want. You will make decisions that will get you closer to driving the car you want to be driving until one day it is in your driveway.

Visualization can work for every object that you want. If you think of it, see it, and put it in front of you every day, you will have it. It is that simple. If you want a larger house someday and define exactly the type of house you would want to have, what color it is outside and inside, what floors it has, what type of kitchen it has, how many bedrooms it has, what kind of bathrooms it has, and then go look at a house like this and put a picture of it somewhere in your house that will make you look at it every day, it is yours. This is a secret that successful, happy, positive people know. They do this often with things that they want. They are not afraid to want things and dream about getting them. Try this with a small object. Find a shirt or an outfit that you want. Or think of a pair of shoes that you want. Maybe you want a new drill or a set of golf clubs. Go look at what you want. Touch it and feel it. Look at the details. Think to yourself how much you would like to have the item. Then find a picture of the item and hang it up in your house. Look at the item every day. You will find yourself wanting the item more and more. Then something will happen. You will begin to focus on how to get that item. You will begin to find ways to have what you want. You will begin to achieve your dream until one day it will be the day that you have the item you wanted.

You can do this with almost anything—a trip to Hawaii for example. You cannot go to Hawaii to see it first, but you can look at pictures, talk to others that have been there, and look at television shows that describe Hawaii and the sights and smells of Hawaii. You can do this with anything. If you hang an item up in your house and tell yourself that you are going to have it someday, it is yours. It does not matter how large or small the item is. The only thing that will change is how long it will take to obtain the item. If you want a boat, it may take two or three years to have. If you want a designer purse, it may only take three or four months to have it. If you want a larger house, it may take you five to ten years to achieve. If you keep your dream in front of you every day, you will have them. Do not be afraid to try this. Do not be afraid to display your pictures of things you want when people come in your house. Be proud that your dreams are defined. Practice this, and see if you do not begin to have the things you want.

Now you know why the name of this book is called, "It's Your Time, It's Your Turn". It's your time now and it's your turn. It's your time to wake up every day with a positive attitude, dreaming of what you want and where you are headed. It' s your turn to be the person that has the big smile on your face all day, stands up tall and smiles with their eyes. It's your time to have positive and fulfilled relationships, to start living the life you always wanted to. It's your time to like your job and enjoy your day. It's your turn to have a positive attitude all the time and to no longer accept negative things in your life but to enjoy every minute and every hour of each day. Life is meant to be lived and it's your time to live it.

CHAPTER 9

Become the Person You Want to Be

Once you begin practicing all the techniques in this book, you are going to begin to feel different. You will begin to look at things and people differently. You may know people that are very negative all the time, and as you become more positive, you will have a hard time relating to them. You may try to talk to them about their negativity, and they may not respond to you. You will not get to the point of being able to sway others to become positive after spending a lifetime of being negative overnight. The same is true if you are very negative all the time suddenly. The positive people in your life would notice it, and most, if not all of them, would probably not respond well to your negativity. From now on, as you begin your journey to becoming a truly positive, happy, successful person, you will be like a duck in the rain. A duck's feathers do not absorb water. When water hits a duck's feathers, it simply rolls off the duck. You must be the same way while embarking on your journey. You cannot let things bother you any longer. When negativity tries to creep back into your life, and it will, you must let it roll off you. Write this down on your piece of paper that you look at every day and night. "Negative things will roll off me like water on a duck, and I will not let them bother me."

As you become more positive, you will find that you will have a shield around you from negativity. As I have described, negativity is all around you, all day long. You have most likely become much more aware of this now that you have read a good portion of this book, but as you read more books and attend positive seminars and years go by, you will see just how much negativity there is around us all the time. I do not mean this in a bad way, and I am not trying to scare you. Negativity is part of life. It is part of our world. The world would not be the place it is without negativity. My goal is to change the world into a positive one, one person at a time. "When you become positive you will pay it forward, when you become negative you will not." That is the power of positive thinking. It is contagious, and it is infectious. Positive thinking is an invisible energy that illuminates from us. It is an energy that makes us feel fantastic, alive, confident, and free. Positive energy makes us feel safe and secure. Positive energy helps us to get in tune with God.

Think for a moment how much different the world would be if it were a positive place and there was no negativity. I say the words "positive" and "negative" to describe how the world would be different, but I really mean, how much different would the world be if everything that positivity achieves happens every day and there is none of what negativity does to the world every day? If there was only positive thinking in the world, it would be a completely different place. I even think that buildings and the way we go through life would be different. Schools would be different. Learning would be different. Schools prepare children for the real world, and well, they should. What if schools spent most of the time teaching children how to become positive and how to tap into their positive energy and did not have to spend so much time teaching them how to enter the real world because the real world was a positive, happy, safe place? Think about if everywhere you went, everyone smiled at one another, talked to one another, always had positive things to say about one another, and helped one another. What if everyone woke up every day, jumped out of bed happy and excited, and looked in the mirror and told themselves "I am so happy to be alive, and I am going to make a difference today in my life and someone's life" or "I am going to be the best person that I can be today, and I am going to smile at people, help people, work hard, and follow my dreams today"? Think about how different cities would be. How different workplaces would be. What if there was no crime, murders, robberies because there is no negativity and no system that created money and the love for objects that money can buy? Think about this for a moment.

This would be a pretty cool place, wouldn't it? If this is how the world looked, I would not have to write this book. But this is not how the world is. I love the world the way it is, and you should too. There is so much positive energy and so many positive people in the world. All we have to do is tap into it and seek out the positive people. Then all we have to do is not allow ourselves to engage in the negativity that negative people throw around. When you become a truly positive person, you will realize that the world will look like a positive place. You will ignore negativity and only notice positive things. You will still have to deal with negative things at your job, at your house, and other places, but your subconscious will be working hard at making you see the positive side of everything, every person, and every situation. Your subconscious will also be working hard to force you to get away from negative situations because you feel uncomfortable in negative situations and will not want to be around them.

As you become more positive and learn to dream and follow your dreams and achieve your dreams, you will become immersed in your own life. Negative people usually do not like their lives, but they cannot figure out why. This is because they are too busy looking at everything from negative eyes. Nothing seems to go their way, and they do not get much accomplished. They are usually unhappy most of the time and cannot figure out why. They do not achieve much and chalk their underachieving up to bad luck. What a way to spin through life. What a way to wake up every day and go to sleep every night. I would not wish this on anyone. Being negative all the time would be like a prison sentence. The good news about negativity is that you can break out of jail anytime you want to. You have the key now to step out of that jail cell and be free to think positive thoughts, achieve your goals, and be truly happy again by achieving a positive attitude. You will begin to like your life more than you ever have. You will start looking at your future. You will start living in the now instead of living in the past. You will think about what happens tomorrow, and you will plan tomorrow.

I always look at the future in my head. I always talk about the future to people I am around. When I am alone, I think to myself what my life will be like five, ten, fifteen years from now. Of course, I have small thoughts of doubt creep up from time to time that say, "You are getting older now. Maybe you will not have the energy you did, and maybe all this dreaming and planning means nothing." And then I just smile, and my subconscious, which knows better, makes me say to myself, "Nonsense, I have seen people in their late sixties and seventies that do nothing and talk negatively." I have had conversations with them. They are miserable, and they know it. They say it. I have also talked to people that are in their late sixties and seventies that are active, happy, and positive and still dream. They are excited about life and happy with themselves and their life. They exercise and enjoy life to the fullest. Who do I want to be? Who do I want to be like when I am older? The answer is simple. Who do you want to be? Who do you want to be like? Who do you want to become?

Because we are human and do not live in a perfect world, I believe that we must spend our entire lives becoming who we want to be. We must do this because as we move through life and take life's journey, we are changing, and things in our lives are changing. Sometimes we make the changes, and sometimes life makes them for us. When life makes them for us, we are forced to react to them and deal with them. While you are going through life from this day forward, just know that it is never too late to become the person you want to be. It is never too late to start. As I get older, I am becoming more excited about my new life I am entering. I am excited that I have recently made the decision to work until the day I die. I am not going to set an alarm, jump in the shower, and drive through morning traffic every day to sit at my desk and work until 5:00 p.m., but I am going to be doing something until the day I die. I will never retire. When we retire, we do just that. Some of the definitions of the word "retire" are "to withdraw, as for rest or seclusion," "to fall back or retreat, as from battle," "to move back or away, recede," "to take out of circulation."

Why would we spend our entire lives moving forward and building a life only to retire at the age of sixty-five? Yes, we will need to slow down and relax a little bit, but I will never retire. And I will never stop becoming the person I want to be. I will never stop dreaming and achieving my goals. My dreams may change when I am older, but I will not stop having them. If you think this way, if you have this perspective about getting older, becoming old is no longer a scary thing. You just get better with age. Do not ever stop becoming who you want to be. If you are reading this book and you are fifty years old, then you have a lot of time to become who you want to be. If you are eight years old and reading this book, you have a lot of time to become who you want to be. If you are twenty and reading this book, then you have a lot of time to become who you want to be. Never use age as an excuse for anything. And never use age as an excuse for becoming positive. Young people could easily read this book and say to themselves, "This kind of stuff is for older people," and older people can easily read this book and say, "This kind of stuff is for younger people." No, this kind of stuff is for all people! It is for everyone, everywhere, all the time in every walk of life. It is a lifestyle and a fantastic way to spend your life! It starts now and ends the day you die. It is that simple. It is never too early or too late to become the person you want to be. The only thing that can get in your way is yourself. Do you understand this? There is only one person that can stop you.

It is very normal if you have an inner battle with yourself as you make the decision to become positive. It is your subconscious telling you that you are programmed differently, but once your subconscious realizes that you are going to reprogram it to become positive all the time, it will work hard to achieve its new goal. You will no longer have that inner struggle. Most people have been thinking about becoming more positive for a while, so when they buy books like this and read them, they are reassuring their subconscious that this is the right way to live, and the inner struggle with becoming positive is much shorter and much less of a struggle. When I think negative thoughts and speak negatively, I begin to have an inner struggle with myself. I do not like it, and I must correct myself. It happens naturally and quickly. The same will happen for you as you become more and more positive. This is perfectly normal, and it happens to everyone. Why do you think there are so many commercials on television about depression? Why are there so many commercials about not sleeping well? They are everywhere, on every channel. Do you think that if the world was a truly positive place, there would be so many depressed people and people that do not sleep well?

I would like to touch on sleep a little bit because sleep can be a positive or negative thing in our lives. Firstly, you need to understand that sleep is very important, but it is something that you must learn to make a positive thing in your life to truly become who you want to be. We spend approximately six to ten hours every day sleeping. If you average that to eight hours per day and you live to seventy-five, that's twenty-five years of sleep or 9,125 days of sleep in your lifetime. If you are going to sleep twenty-five years of your life if you live to seventy-five, then don't you think you should look at sleep as a positive thing? The most important thing that you should know about sleep is that from this day forward, you need to look at sleep as something positive that you must do every day or night. If you do not, then you need to change your perspective of sleep and sleeping. I have never slept well my entire life. My sisters tell me that when I was a baby, I did not sleep well. They say that I "never slept." I do wish that I never had to sleep. How much more could we get accomplished if we did not have to sleep? If every human being that lived to seventy-five had twenty-five more years to be awake, dreaming and achieving, how different would the world be?

This is not how the world is though. The fact of the matter is that all species on planet Earth must sleep and rest. It is how the world goes around. Knowing this, it is important that sleep becomes a positive thing in your life. Some self-help books will talk about sleep.

Most will say get into a habit every night that will help you sleep. This is true, and it does help. They will also say that you should go to bed at the same time every night and make your bedroom a nice place that you want to sleep in. This is true also. They say that you should get into a routine that you do every night, like brushing your teeth and washing your face before bed. This is also true. They say that you should have a comfortable bed because if you are going to spend an average of eight hours per day on it, you should be comfortable. This is true too. Every night before I go to bed, I try to do the same thing. I brush my teeth, wash my face, and put on pajamas. I lie in bed, turn the television on and find a show that relaxes me, and then clear my mind and relax until I fall asleep. Most people that talk about sleeping will tell you not to watch television before going to bed, and they are right, but that is what works for me. You should find out what works for you. Try different things before you go to bed to see what relaxes you and what helps you sleep well.

I believe that people make too big of a deal out of sleep. Sleep to me is a requirement in life that we all must do. It is that simple. It is important to sleep, but my world does not revolve around sleep. If I do not sleep well, I do not get stressed out over it. This is partly because I have not slept well my entire life, but I have also had times when I have slept perfectly also. I know the difference between sleeping well and not sleeping well. If you do not sleep well, just know that many people in the world do not sleep well. Many successful, happy, positive people do not sleep well. You should spend time learning how to get enough sleep to make you feel good because sleep is a positive thing for your body and mind, but you should not make sleeping well a negative experience. I often wake up around 3:00 a.m. Sometimes I fall right back asleep, and sometimes I stay awake for two hours. I do not stress out about this, and I do not make it a negative experience. I sometimes will have negative thoughts when I wake up at 3:00 a.m. and try to go back to sleep, but I spend the rest of my time in bed turning those negative thoughts into positive ones. If I have a hard time thinking positive thoughts at 3:00 a.m., I simply roll over and turn the television on, find a relaxing show to watch, and clear my mind. After a while, I get sleepy again and doze back off. This works for me, but it may not work for you. You should concentrate on ways to get a good night's rest.

I read a book about sleep many years ago, and it talked about some interesting studies that have been done about sleep. One study that stuck out to me was a study that was done on a seventy-five-year-old woman. This lady did not sleep more than four hours per night her entire life. She was extremely healthy and told the people doing the study that she did not feel tired and sleeping four hours per night did not affect her life one bit. The book was basically about the difference between sleeping disorders and normal sleeping habits. The book talked about how some people really do have a sleeping disorder, but then some people just do not sleep good sometimes. A sleeping disorder is when you do not sleep one night, and then you do not sleep the next night and maybe even a third or fourth night. When you have a sleeping disorder, this happens often. Everything is affected when you have a sleeping disorder. Your job performance is affected, your concentration is affected, your attitude is affected, and basically your life is affected by it. When you just do not sleep well sometimes, it is not a sleeping disorder. If you have a hard time sleeping one night and feel tired at work and then go to bed early that night when you get home, just know that everyone has that problem sometimes. And when I say everyone, I mean just about everyone. We all have problems sleeping sometimes. I am only mentioning this because I have not slept well my entire life, and I have learned not to make it a negative force in my life. It is just how I am. It does not matter if I am stressed out or not, tired or not, or anything else. It is just something that happens to me. If you do not sleep well, hopefully this will help you to not make it a negative thing. As a matter of fact, if you do not sleep as much as most people, you should think of it as a very positive thing. I have learned to love the fact that I do not require eight hours of sleep per night. If I only need six to seven hours of sleep per night, then that means I have seven to fourteen hours per week more of waking hours to achieve my dreams and to do things that I enjoy doing. I turned not sleeping well into a positive thing. I also get to relax and watch television shows I record or read a book in the middle of the night while other people are sleeping. I think about my life and my dreams in a positive manner and all the things I want to achieve in the middle of the night. I think of other people in my life in a positive manner and I get to program my positive attitude in the middle of the night when I cannot sleep. I never make the times I cannot sleep at night negative. I always turn them into positive times. That is positive for me. Do not make sleep a negative factor in your life. Make it a positive one.

I read one time in a book that even if you do not sleep a lot of hours, it is important to get quality sleep. This is something you can control. You should make your bedroom a place that you want to be in eight hours per day. The colors of the walls, the pictures on the walls, your bedroom furniture, the covering on the windows in your bedroom should all be things that make you happy. All these things should make you feel good. The kind of flooring should be the type that you like because you are always in your room, and most of the time, we walk barefoot in our bedroom. You should be comfortable when you are barefoot in your bedroom. Your bed should be very comfortable to you. Your bathroom should be pleasant and comfortable. You should have nice towels in your bathroom and new towels. All these things add up to make your time in your bedroom better and to psychologically make you feel better about sleep. This will also help you to sleep better and deeper. If you tell yourself every night before you go to bed that you hate your room, the furniture, your bed is uncomfortable, your closet is too small and cluttered, you hate the furniture in y out bedroom, your bathroom is not organized how you would like it, and so on, what does that do to your attitude? That is negative. You must be honest with yourself if you feel that way, so there is only one way to turn your bedroom into a positive place. Spend time making it that way. Start today. You do not have to spend a lot of money, but do some things right away to make you feel good about your bedroom. When you go to bed at night, you should feel happy before bed, and you should feel good in your bedroom.

As you become more positive, you are going to realize that you have more energy. As you have been observing positive, happy, successful people, have you noticed how much energy they have? This is not a coincidence. This does not happen by chance. Positive energy is thoughts in positive motion, and negative energy is thoughts in negative motion. When you think negative thoughts, you will find that you have less energy. This is because your thoughts do not involve any motion when they are negative. When you have positive thoughts and dreams, your subconscious will force you to put your thoughts into motion, which will give you more energy. Take advantage of this. Get in tune with your inner energy. Your inner energy is what will help you achieve your dreams and become more positive. Your inner energy is what will make you happier and attract positive energy from others and from the world around you. You will find as you become more positive that you will not sleep as much. You will not feel as tired as you used to. You will be more excited about life. Use this energy to your advantage. When you feel this energy, do not ignore it, but instead, pay attention to it and relish in this positive energy. It will make you crave more of it. You will become hooked on the awesome feeling you will have from your positive energy. Remember that life is meant to be lived, and you should spend your short time on earth enjoying each day as if it was your last.

When you practice all the techniques in this book, you can achieve a state of euphoria. You will feel something that you have never felt before. It is like what they describe while doing drugs, but with the side effect of only making you feel better and better. If you think positive thoughts all day, have positive conversations with yourself, exercise, eat right, have happy, loving relationships, keep your money affairs in order and have some savings to fall back on, and dream and achieve your dreams, how do you think your life will be? Take a moment and think about this. You have put this book down along the way while reading it and thought about each of these individually, but now it is time to put the book down and think about all of them together. Think about how your life will be when you are doing all this each day. Each week, each month, and each year, year in and year out, for the rest of your life. I can tell you because I do this. It is fantastic!

Think about how different your life is going to become. Now put the book down, close your eyes for a few minutes, and vision yourself doing all these things. Tell yourself that you are going to do this and that you are going to achieve all the things that this book has taught you and that you are going to work on all the things that you are already doing that you have read in this book. Tell yourself that you are awesome and that you are going become the person that you want to be and have the things in life that you want. Think to yourself, talk to yourself, and be proud of who you are and who you are going to become. Give yourself a mental pat on the back for wanting to grow and wanting to be positive. Do it now.

You are now on the way to a much more fulfilled life. You are like a budding plant that will open on a sunny day and soak all the sun in. As you practice all the techniques in this book, do not be surprised if you hunger for more knowledge. When you do, make sure that you feed your hunger. You will crave more positive literature, conversations, and positive energy around you. Do not be surprised when this happens. A positive attitude is something that must be nurtured and practiced every day. You should start now and begin to find more positive literature. See if there are any positive seminars coming to your city or a city near you in the next twelve months. If there is, commit to it now. Sign up for it, and pay for it so it is on your calendar. Just show up for it. All the great feelings you have had while reading this book will all come back to you, and you will learn new and exciting techniques and tricks to become positive. If you only get one thing out of the seminar, it was worth it. But I bet you will get many, many things out of it. There is something else that happens at a positive-thinking seminar. You will see many other people that are like-minded. You will see that there are many, many people in your city and in cities near you that think positive and are changing their lives. You will feel incredible knowing that you are not alone but are among others that are just like you. You will realize that you are not crazy and that all the amazing things that you are feeling are valid, and other people are doing the same thing as you. After you attend a positive seminar, you will realize that many people all around you are reading books to become positive and practicing positive thinking every day. People that you know are doing this. It is happening all around, and you will be more aware of it as time goes by.

Do not think that you are going to become someone that you are not or someone different. You are going to be the same person you are, but now you are going to be better. You can dream again and feel happy all the time. All your morals and beliefs will stay the same. When you have free time to do things you like, make sure that you are doing things such as listening to music, going to a concert or a movie. Maybe you like to fish or sew or knit. Whatever it is that you like that makes you happy and makes you feel good, start doing more of it. Try to set a little time aside for yourself to do the things you like. If you are married or in a relationship, then sit down with your mate and talk about some things that you like to do together. If you already know what these things are, then plan to do them. Life can get very hectic, and we sometimes forget to do the things we like.

The things that you like to do not have to involve money. Maybe you used to like to go to the park on a nice day with your mate when you first met and lie in the grass together and look at the sky and talk. If you like that, then go do that again. When the next nice day comes that you both can go to the park, do it. Schedule it into your month. Do not wait. Maybe you like going to concerts, and you have not been to one in many years. If so, buy tickets for a concert that is coming to your city that you would like to go to. If you buy the tickets now and the concert is two or three weeks away, you will have something to look forward to. Maybe you like to get together with your family. Call your family members and plan a day that everyone gets together in the next two or three weeks. Plan something nice. Make a theme for it, like Mardi Gras, a Hawaiian theme, or a theme that your family would like. Make the food that everyone brings and cooks that day part of the theme. This will give you something positive that makes you feel good, something to look forward to, and something to plan. These are all positive things. The more positive things that you must think about and do, things that make you feel good, the less time you will have to spend on negative thoughts and negative activities.

Take a minute to enjoy your life. Take a minute to celebrate how good life is with yourself. That is right. You can have a celebration with yourself. Celebrate the life you have and the life you are going to have. When you celebrate your life and think of the past, always think of your past as a stepping-stone to where you are now. Realize that your life is going to be full of stepping-stones from this day forward, and you have control of the stepping-stones you create. Know that there are no wrong decisions, just decisions. Something good will come out of every stepping-stone you create. Have faith in God that your stepping-stones in the past and in the future are leading you to something wonderful. You now have the key to the vehicle that can get you where you want to be. All you have to do is get in and start driving. I like to think of life as a journey. You will read some materials and sayings that say, "Life is a journey." Life really is a journey. The definition of the word "journey" is "an act or instance of traveling from one place to another." As we move through our journey of life, we need to realize that we can either enjoy the ride or be miserable on the ride.

It is time to look at your life. Look at your journey up until this point. Then look at where you are headed on your journey of life. Take time to look at your future in your head and to start planning your future. "What the mind sees, it will achieve." Look at yourself years from now. Picture how you want to be, how you want your relationships to be, and how you want your children to be two, five, ten, fifteen years from now. Do not be afraid to think this far in the future. When you think about your life years from now, let your mind go. Think about details that you want for yourself. Think about what kind of house you would like to live in, what the kitchen will look like, what the colors of the walls will be, what your furniture will look like. Think about all the details that you want in the future. Do not be afraid to dream and to dream about many years in the future. Now you know that not all dreams do come true, and there are many things that can alter your dreams and change your dreams along the journey of achieving them. All this is part of life, and it is all part of the journey. All this is a positive thing and not negative. Do not be afraid to make your life what you want it to be now. It is time to become the person you want to be.

Chapter 10

Make The Decision To Do It

The definition of the word "decision" is "the passing of judgment of an issue under consideration," "the act of reaching a conclusion or making up one's mind." Now that you know all that you have learned in this book and you have been practicing it for a while, it is time to decide to become a positive person. Once you decide to do something, there is literally nothing that can stop you. A decision is one of the most powerful things that human beings do. Once you decide to become a positive person, you will know that you have done it. You may have done this already, but if you have not, here is how you will know. All the techniques that you have practiced in this book become clear to you. You will know exactly where you are headed and what you want. Until you decide to change and do what it takes to achieve all that you have learned in this book, you will not truly become positive. You will not be able to overcome some of the hurdles and obstacles that life will throw at you along your journey. But once you decide to where you are going, you will become unstoppable.

Once you decide to change your life, you will realize that nothing can stand in your way. Nothing else will matter except your dream to become the person you want to be and have the things in life that you want. When you have a clear dream and the tools to achieve it and then make a decision to do it, you will light all the fires inside of you, and you will attract all the positive energy needed from other people, the world, and the universe. This is how you will know that you have decided to change your life. You will feel a huge difference in yourself, and everyone around you will see it. It is important that you decide to become achieve a truly positive attitude. There is only one technique that you must learn now to be on your way to having a truly happy, successful, fulfilling, and positive life. You must learn how to make a decision. You are going to have to decide if you really want everything that I have talked about in this book. You must believe that all this will make a difference in your life and that you are worth it. You must believe that it really is your time and that it really is your turn. You must decide to go forward and keep practicing all these techniques day in and day out. You cannot miss a day to read your piece of paper that you have made. Read it every morning and every night, and carry a copy of it with you. Look at your dreams every day, and tell yourself that you are going to have them. Make new dreams for yourself and new goals, and do not be afraid to dream. Add to your piece of paper that you look at every morning and every night. Change it and make it your own as time goes by. Keep the things on it that you have written down so far that you like the most, and then add your own thoughts, sayings, and ideas to your list.

The most important decision you are going to have to make is to keep learning more techniques and practicing the techniques that all the happy, successful, positive people around the world practice every day. Read more books, listen to CDs, attend seminars, watch positive television shows, hang around positive people, and make your home a positive home. Make your workday a positive work day. Decide to reprogram your subconscious to help you become a positive, happy person and to help you get all the things in life that you want and can dream about. You will make many decisions every day of your life. Tell yourself that you are going to decide to eat the right kind of foods that you know are healthy for you. There is no secret about what foods are healthy. The secret to eating healthy is to be able to make the decision that you are going to do it every day. Decide that you are going to exercise, and that your goal is to be exercising at least five times per week eventually.

As we go through life, there are always windows and doors opening and closing all around us. There are opportunities and decisions that we make that will lead us down different paths, depending on those decisions we make. Decide that you are going to make the correct decision every time and that no matter what decision you make, something good will come out of it, and every decision you make will be the right one. Decide to ask God to guide you on every path and lead you in every decision you make. From this day forward, there are no wrong decisions for you any longer. There are only decisions, and they are always correct. You may not know why now, but you will know why later. Know that something good will come out of every decision. All you have to do is keep looking for it.

When you are making the decision to become the person you want to be and to have the things that you want in life, always make it a positive experience. Never be hard on yourself. You must learn to enjoy the journey now and to enjoy the decisions you make in life. Learn to trust yourself and to trust others around you. Never ask advice on a major decision, especially about achieving a truly positive attitude. When you are making decisions, consult with yourself. Talk to yourself, think to yourself, and most importantly, listen to your gut. Your gut will never lie. Take as long as you need to make decisions. Wait until your gut tells you what to do. When you feel your gut tell you what the right decision about something is, you will know that your subconscious has spoken and that you are on the right path. You will also know that God has spoken. Know that no matter what the outcome of a decision you make is, there is some reason that you made that decision. You may not find out for a long time, even years later, why something good came of a decision you have made, but you will always find out. When you make decisions from a positive perspective, you will see that you cannot fail. There is no bad that comes from positive decisions. It may seem like something bad has happened, but it is only a hurdle or a stepping-stone to get to where you are headed.

I have learned to trust all these things I am describing when I make decisions or even while bad things are happening to me. I have had situations in my life where something negative has happened to me and has even lasted for years. No matter what the negative situation was throwing at me, I simply had to remember a few things. I had to tell myself that it was going to be all right over and repeatedly. In some cases, I had to do this for years about the same situation. Every time I would think about the situation, I would not engage in negative thoughts with myself. I would simply tell myself that it was going to be all right and think about something positive. But saying that it was going to be all right was not enough. I had to make the decision to believe that it was going to be all right. I had to realize that something good was going to come out of what was happening to me. That is sometimes easier said than done, isn't it? But once you do this one time and then see that something good comes from every bad situation, you will never look at a negative situation the same way. You will then be able to deal with anything that life throws at you. You will think of challenges and negative things that come your way as speed bumps and not roadblocks.

Doesn't everything I have described in this book sound fantastic? Does this sound like a fantasy or a dream? Striving to have a perfect life, having the things that you want in life. Being happy all the time. Thinking and saying positive thoughts all the time. Exercising, eating right, and looking and feeling fantastic every day! It almost sounds too good to be true, doesn't it? I assure you it is not, and it is attainable. It all starts with a decision though. It all starts with you telling yourself that you are going to do it, and do it now! You must make the decision to believe that you deserve it. You must make the decision that you are going to do what it takes, no matter how long it takes. You must believe everything that you are reading on the piece of paper you have made while reading this book. When you read it every morning, throughout the day, and before you go to bed, you must believe every word of it. You must decide that this is what you really want. You must decide that you are going to make it happen. The decision is yours and nobody else's. This is your life, and now you are going to take control of it and live it the way you want to. Think of it as jumping on a horse that is wild and taking the reins and riding that horse until it submits, and you have full control of the horse. You are in control of your life now.

Once you decide about something, never look back and always look forward. Put your positive glasses on when you decide so you can see the path clearly. Once you decide to do something, do it! Just go for it once you decide about something. If you have decided to become the person that you want to be and you believe that it is your time and it is your turn, then go for it! When you decide about something, you will realize that nothing else matters. Once you decide that you are going to do something, your dreams will come true. It all starts with you—a decision, a dream, and positive energy. When you combine this and ask God to guide you, you cannot fail. And if you do not obtain your dreams right away, it is only because there is something bigger and better that is in store for you. Always know from this day forward that there is a reason for everything that happens to you. There are no wrong decisions, only decisions that will lead you to achieving your goals and dreams faster.

Once you decide to become the person that you want to be, have confidence. Confidence is something that all positive, happy, successful people have. Confidence is what makes others around you know that you are in control of your life. But more importantly, confidence is what lets you know that you are in control of your life. The definition of confidence is "a feeling of consciousness of one's powers or of reliance on one's circumstances," "faith or belief that one will act in a right, proper or effective way," "the quality or state of being certain." Learn to believe in yourself now. Learn to trust yourself now. Now that you know there are factors in your body, mind, and soul that make you who you are and you know how to use them, have confidence that you are on the right path. Did you ever think that maybe you are not reading this book by coincidence? Maybe there is a reason you are reading this book. I am sure that you have already thought of this, but if you have not, take a moment to think about it. Have confidence in you. Have confidence in what you have achieved in life so far and what you want to achieve in the future. "Learn from the past, but focus on the future." Know where you are headed. Have confidence in your abilities.

Once you decide that you are going to become the person that you want to be, stand up tall, lift your head, put your shoulders back, and walk proudly. Smile all the time and laugh often. Smile with your eyes, and look people in the eye. Show your confidence, and show others that you are confident. Do not hold it back. When you feel confident, act confident and show it. Let others around you know that you are serious. Decide that it's your time and it's your turn. Let yourself know by how you act that you are confident. When you are sitting down, sit up straight. When you breathe, take deep breaths, and inhale all the positive energy around you while exhaling the negative energy. You must decide to do all these things. We all have so many decisions to make that have either a negative or positive effect on you. They all add up one way or another. Tip the scale to the positive side, and then overflow it with positiveness so it slams down to the positive side. Decide that everything you do is going to add to the positive side of your scale. If negativity starts piling up on the negative side of your scale and tipping it back, just brush it off, and you will see that the scale starts moving back to the positive side again. Your goal is to keep your negative scale weighed completely down with positive decisions that you are making each day. Make all your decisions end up on the positive side of your scale.

Make sure you dress for success. When you feel like you look good, you feel good. If you have old clothes that are faded or just do not look good any longer, then it is time to change that. It is time to decide that you are going to look good all the time. How you feel about yourself is everything. When you look in the mirror with no clothes on, it is just as important as how you feel when you look in the mirror with clothes on. When you dress to go anywhere or do anything, make sure you feel good about the way you look. If it is time to update your wardrobe, then put that down on your list of goals. If you cannot afford new clothes right now, then simply make it a goal to have new clothes. Having new clothes and looking great is a positive thing. You wear clothes every day of your life, and sometimes you change into different outfits throughout the day. Make sure that your clothes match when you get dressed. If you do not know much about clothes, then read magazines about fashion or look on the Internet about how people are dressing currently. Take time to learn about fashion and how to dress. Ask a friend that knows about fashion to help you. You do not have to look like everyone else. Be yourself, but make sure you dress for success! Learn how to put an outfit together and how to match your clothes. Once you get the hang of it, you will not believe how easy it is. There are certain basics to dressing that will make a huge difference in the way you look. If your clothes are old and faded and are yesterday's styles, what will that say about you? Even if you do not feel this way, that is what you will be saying with your clothes. If you are dressed for success and having a bad day, this will tell others that you are confident, positive, and successful, no matter what life is throwing at you.

If you are a construction worker, then do not worry about how you look during work, but if you are a supervisor at a construction company, then your appearance means everything. If you are a construction worker, treat yourself to having some nice clothes in your closet and in your drawers for times when you go out and do the things that you like to do or while you get together with friends or family. Always look and feel positive whenever you get the chance to. This will tell yourself that you believe in yourself and that you are positive, and you believe that you deserve to look and feel good. This will also tell others the same thing.

Look at the people that you have been observing that are happy, positive, and successful. Do they do all the things described in this chapter? Do they stand up tall and walk proudly? Do they look at people in their eyes? Do they dress nicely? Are they dressed for success? I bet they are. I bet they do all these things that I have described in this chapter. If you are not doing these things every day and night, then it is time to make the decision to change. It is time for you to feel incredible! You have all this inside of you. We all do. It is just waiting to be unleashed. That is what truly happy, positive, successful people know that others do not. They know how to unleash their positive energy.

Once you practice all these techniques and understand how they all work together, you will be much more apt to take risks. Risks will not scare you any longer, and you will look at risks as positive things. I bet when you see the word "risk," you think of it as a negative word and a negative thing. "Risk" is a positive word, and taking risks are positive actions. "Without risk, there is no reward." Sometimes you must take risks to get to where you want to be. Remember this: there is no successful person on this planet that has not taken a risk. Everything that is worth doing has some risk involved in it. When you start taking more risks, you will start getting more rewards. Once you learn to overcome the fears of taking risks, you will no longer feel that you are not living your life the fullest. You will feel that if you decide to do something, nothing will be able to stand in your way. When you dream, you will no longer be afraid to go after your dreams because you will not be afraid of the obstacles and risks of achieving your dreams. The only reason you will not go after your dreams is because you make the decision not to, not because you are afraid of the risks involved in achieving them. You will have the confidence to know that you are going to be able to achieve your goals and dreams. Put the book down now and get your piece of paper that you read every day. Write down that you are confident and that you are not afraid to take risks. Write down that others will know that you are confident and that you have decided to become the person that you want to be and to have all the things in life that you want.

After you are done reading this book, put it in a safe place. Put it somewhere that you will be able to remember where it is and a place where it will not accidentally get thrown away. Then six months or a year from now, read this book again. You may have forgotten some things that you will have wanted to practice. You will also read other things that you missed the first time you read this book. You will read things that you completely did not see the first time. That is how you will know that you are going to get the most out of this book, by reading it again. Keep the book to refer to as years go by. You may open this book two years from now and remember a chapter as you look at the book and remember that you should be practicing a technique you read two years ago or more. Do this with all the books that you read about a positive attitude or self-help from now on. Just by looking at them every so often, you will remember the specific message that a book had in it and what message you got from the book. I do this often with the books I have. I will just look at them as time goes by, and I will remember what I got out of the book and what I learned from the book. Every book you read will have a different twist on how to get to where you want to be in life. This is because every author's journey has been different, and the paths they have chosen to have led them to the same place, but the way they got there was not the same.

As time goes by, you will begin to develop your own beliefs, feelings, and strategies on how you, the world, and the universe work. You will begin to feel things that you have never felt before, and you will be able to sense things that you never have. You will become more in tune with all the positive energy around you at all times. When this happens, just know that it is perfectly natural. It is what you want to happen. It is what the happy, successful, positive people know that you do not. This will happen subtly and gradually most likely. You are not going to wake up one day and be a completely different person. You are not going to be a different person ever. You will always remain who you are inside, but now you can also become the person that you want to be. You get to pick and choose what you want out of life. You will no longer feel like a tiny boat drifting in the ocean with no direction and not knowing where land is. Instead, you will feel like a marathon runner taking off from the start line and knowing exactly what pace you are going to run at, how long it will take to finish the race, and where the finish line is. You will never settle for second best again.

As you become the person you want to be, you will notice that you will become much more trusting and curious about other people and other cultures. You will want to learn more about what other cultures are thinking and practicing about being truly positive. You will discover that all other cultures practice being truly positive, but the only difference is that they may practice it from a different perspective. It does not matter what culture you are; this will hold true for all cultures. Remember, we are all taking different paths to get to the same place. Embrace other cultures, and take the time to learn about other cultures. Every culture has positive energy, and every culture knows what positive thinking is. When people are different, it can make us feel uncomfortable. Learn to love that people are different, and know that it is what makes humans human and the earth what it is. Remember though that under our skin, humans are all the same. We are one species. Our environments and cultures may have made us look different on the outside, but on the inside, we are basically the same. Our basic needs for survival are the same. Always make sure you respect every race and culture. When you do this, you will be practicing positive thinking that will make you feel good. The dislike of other cultures or of people that are different from you is a very negative thing. Make sure that you eliminate any of these thoughts or feelings.

One thing that I like to do is to eat foods from other cultures. Food is a universal subject that all people and all nationalities like to talk about. Talk about food with people you know from different cultures. Eat their foods if you get a chance. When you break bread with people, you will see that it makes everyone comfortable with each other. Every country looks at cooking and eating food as a social event. When you eat another culture's food with someone of that culture, you tell them that you accept them and that you respect them. This is very positive, and it will make you feel good. Whenever I get to know someone from another country or from another culture, I always talk about what kinds of foods they eat. I ask them what spices they use while cooking, what ingredients they use, and how their foods taste compared to the foods I eat all the time. I love to eat foods that people from other cultures have cooked. It makes them feel so proud and good, and it makes me feel good also. Try this sometime, and you will see how much of a positive experience it is. You will also see how different you feel about other cultures and how much you will realize that we are all basically the same inside.

We have differences, but we are all humans, and we are all after our goals and dreams. When you eat with someone, you talk about things that you will not talk about any other time. When you are eating a meal with someone, you will relax and talk about intimate things, and huge walls come down, which allows people to have much different conversations and build trust among themselves that cannot be done in a professional or social setting.

As you learn more and more about being a truly positive person and make the decision to become more and more positive, make sure that you pay it forward. Positive thinking is something that can change the world. If I could waive a wand and make the world a completely positive place, I would. Being positive is not something that they teach in schools. There were no positive-thinking classes or classes that specifically talked about how to become a positive, happy, successful person when I was growing up. There are no college classes that are based on positive thinking. But you will soon discover that thinking positive thoughts and speaking positive words is the key to everything in life. As you learn more about becoming positive and practice more techniques that you learn and develop by yourself, share your ideas and what you have learned with others. You will find that once you talk about being positive with people, being positive is something that all people want to know about and talk about. You will see that everyone is talking about being positive with other people. The only reason people do not openly discuss it is because they do not want people to think they are different or weird. Once you feel comfortable talking about being truly positive, you will see that people are fascinated with the idea of being truly positive, but they do not know how to achieve it or where to begin. Help others, and share what you learn. Share your ideas and the things that you try on your own that work for you to become truly positive. Pay it forward!

It has been my extreme honor to have been able to share my ideas and knowledge with you and to know that I may have helped you in some way to become the person you want to be and have all of the things in your lifetime you desire. I am humbled to know that I may have helped you to achieve your goals and dreams in life. I am very excited to think that I may have helped you to become a truly positive person. "What I know as a coach means nothing, what I can impart to you as a coach means everything." Hopefully, you will never be the same after reading this book. I can only hope that you will learn how to achieve all your goals and dreams in life. I can only hope that you will feel what it is like to be a truly positive person with a truly positive attitude. Only you can make that decision. Only you can make that happen! You are the reason I have written this book. I congratulate, salute, and applaud you for reading this book and only ask that you read more books like this and attend seminars on positive thinking. Never stop learning and practicing being positive. Make that decision for yourself. You owe it to yourself. Then make the decision to help others that think negative thoughts but would like to change. Pay it forward and become the person helping others.

I have had people share their ideas and thoughts with me throughout my lifetime. This has happened because I was brave enough to tell people that I wanted to become a truly positive person, and I was not afraid to talk about it. I have had people suggest books throughout my life that they have read and suggest seminars that they have attended. I have always read the books that were suggested to me and have attended any seminar I could about positive thinking that was suggested to me by others. I have listened to many tapes and CDs about positive thinking and self-help techniques. Become a person that does the same thing. Do not keep yourself a secret! Let the world know who you are, and let your sphere of influence know who you are. Dare to dream, and dare to achieve. And most importantly, dare to make the decision to achieve a truly positive attitude and to become the person you want to be because it's your time and it's your turn!

NOTES

NOTES

NOTES

NOTES

NOTES

Quotes

"What you believe, you will achieve." Sonny Martell

"I can change whatever I want to." Sonny Martell

"Liking yourself the way you are is the number one goal in life." Sonny Martell

"You are only as good as the company you keep." Unknown

"You are what you eat." Anthelme Brillat-Savarin

"You are what you put into your brain." Sonny Martell

"Talking to yourself is a sign of high intelligence." Sonny Martel

"What you think, you will achieve." Unknown

"Challenges get you up." Unknown

"Motivation is what gets you started, habit is what keeps you going." Jim Rohn

"I am human, and I am not perfect." Sonny Martell

"Every morning in Africa, a gazelle wakes up. It knows it must run faster than the fastest lion or it will be killed. . . Every morning a lion wakes up. It knows it must out run the slowest gazelle or it will starve to death. It doesn't matter whether you are a lion or a gazelle . . . When the sun comes up, you'd better be running." Unknown

"I look at money as a positive thing, and I do not worry about what other people have. I only worry about what I have and what I want that money can buy." Sonny Martell

"I will have all the things in life that I want and all the money I want in time." Sonny Martell

"I will do what it takes to achieve this, and I will think positive thoughts and enjoy the journey while achieving my goals that involve money and what money can buy." Sonny Martell

"It is better to have loved and lost than to never have loved at all." Alfred Lord Tennyson

"I will make my relationship with my mate positive, happy, and loving." Sonny Martell

"Consistency is the hobgoblin of dull minds and relationships." Unknown

"Taking a dream to a reality is a process." Sonny Martell

"You have to feed your own ego all of the time so you can be what you want to be." Sony Martell

"If you don't take risks, how can you change the world?" Sonny Martell

"Realize that everyone has doubts and fears, not just you. It's what you do about them and how you handle them that counts." Sonny Martell

"Don't let age stand in your way." Unknown

"You have to be a problem solver." Unknown

"Show me a good loser, and I will show you a loser." Vince Lombardi

"You have to believe you are the best, but it doesn't mean you are better." Unknown

"Part-time effort will result in part-time results." Unknown

"Make a decision to achieve what you believe." Sonny Martell

"Every thought kept ever constant leads to action and results follow thoughts determine what you want. Action determines what you get, and action is thought in motion." Unknown

"Negative things will roll off me like water on a duck, and I will not let them bother me." Sonny Martell

"What the mind sees, it will achieve." Unknown

"Dress for success." Unknown

"Without risk, there is no reward." Unknown

"Pay it forward." Unknown

"What I know as a coach means nothing, what I can impart to you as a coach means everything." Unknown

"It's your time, it's your turn." Sonny Martell

"The more dreams and risks a person makes in their lives, the more dreams they will achieve" Sonny martell

About the Author

Sonny Martell has studied and developed the techniques and effects of achieving a positive attitude his entire life. Sonny has helped hundreds of people discover how their lives could improve in every aspect by understanding how to implement simple techniques to achieve a positive attitude. Sonny has spent a lifetime practicing and teaching the techniques he has learned to others to grow successful businesses with a culture of positive people helping others. Sonny speaks to groups of all kinds to help them understand and implement the techniques he has developed in order to enhance their personal and financial lives. It is Sonny's goal to make the world a more positive place by assisting everyone in improving their lives and achieving any goal they set by learning the simple techniques he shares in this book.

Printed in the United States
By Bookmasters